# IDEAS AND
# ISSUES
# IN PRIMARY ELT

Edited by

**Chris Kennedy and
Jennifer Jarvis**

Nelson

**In association with
the Centre for British Teachers**

Thomas Nelson and Sons Ltd
Nelson House Mayfield Road
Walton-on-Thames Surrey
KT12 5PL UK

51 York Place
Edinburgh
EH1 3JD UK

Thomas Nelson (Hong Kong) Ltd
Toppan Building 10/F
22A Westlands Road
Quarry Bay Hong Kong

© The Centre for British Teachers 1991

First published by Thomas Nelson and Sons Ltd 1991

ISBN 0-17-556265-2

NPN 9 8 7 6 5 4 3 2 1

Printed in Hong Kong.

# Contents

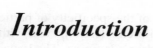

# *Introduction*

The Conference at which these papers were first presented brought together people concerned with many different aspects of teaching English to primary-age learners. It was the first opportunity many of us had had to share ideas with so many colleagues from different work contexts. This book reflects the sense of sharing and excitement which were evident at the Conference.

One of the most significant facts about the young learner field is its diversity. The case studies in this book, particularly in Part 1 *Asking the Questions and Providing the Answers* and Part 3 *Curriculum and Syllabus Design*, present perspectives from Asia, Africa, and Europe. Each raises critical questions about the transferability of ideas from one context to another. The articles are often refreshingly non-doctrinaire, in that the central importance of each particular context is stressed, and the authors present their struggles to relate ideas about teaching children and children's learning to the specific constraints they face. No one approach can be seen as a panacea; instead we get an illuminating sense of 'work in progress' from which we can make comparisons with our own teaching situations and seek new perspectives.

Unlike programmes for adults, language programmes for children cannot often be justified from the perspective of the learners' 'needs' for English. Instead, the teaching/learning situation itself often has to provide the motivation for learning. This has led to two further issues of fundamental importance in this book. The first is an underlying search for an understanding of how children learn, and of the ELT implications of this understanding. Several writers, for example, have found help in the pioneering work of Margaret Donaldson (1979). She has suggested the power in children's learning of their experience of human intention and reasons for doing things. Children rely on this experience to help them make sense of the new. The meaningfulness of story, for example, can be understood in relation to story's power to embody human intention, in situations which support and explain it. Many of the papers in Part 2 *Teaching: Influences and Ideas*, and Part 4 *Language in the Classroom*, explore ideas for utilising children's ways of making sense so that learning is more meaningful and purposeful for them. The papers suggest realisations, in specific teaching contexts, for **meaningfulness** and **purposefulness** in English Language Teaching.

The second underlying issue focuses on the teacher. It is the issue of how the teacher can *support* children's learning; knowing when and how to support and when to relinquish control to the child. The teacher's job is therefore seen as dependent on awareness of the issues of learning underlying most of the papers in the book. Some kinds of support are discussed in Part 4 *Language in the Classroom*, where the focus is on how the teacher can use language to generate meaningful interaction in the classroom, and on how children can be supported in doing the tasks before them. In Part 5 *Teacher Training and Development*, approaches in teacher training are presented, again from perspectives sharpened by the constraints of specific situations. Particular emphasis is given to discovering the teachers' own perceptions of their role and teaching situation, and using these to help them develop further. Through this, teacher training can be seen to replicate understandings important in children's learning.

This book is concerned with issues of the specificity of particular contexts; with developing understandings of children's learning; and with generating techniques of teacher-support for children's learning. The issues are ones which confront most of us involved in teaching English to primary-age learners. We hope that the papers in this book will convey something of the interest and illumination we can gain from the ideas of colleagues who also grapple with the issues.

Chris Kennedy
Jennifer Jarvis
1990

# *A note on the Leeds conference*

In July 1989 The Centre for British Teachers (CBT) in collaboration with the British Association for Applied Linguistics (BAAL) organised a conference in Leeds as part of CBT's 21st Anniversary celebrations. CBT had been involved in a large-scale educational project at primary level for a number of years and it seemed appropriate to choose 'Primary English Language Teaching' as a theme.

Participation was international and 30 papers were given during the two-and-a-half days of the Conference. This Collection is an attempt to represent the major issues that were raised at the Conference, and it is hoped that the articles will provide a useful resource for those working in the field.

Chris Kennedy

# Part 1
## Asking the questions and providing the answers

### Introduction

All three writers in Part 1 of this Collection raise the fundamental question of whether a second language should be taught to younger children. Brumfit concludes that there appear to be no strong theoretical reasons for not teaching children a second language. He warns, however, that there may be practical constraints on implementing teaching programmes if the needs of the teachers are not met, particularly those relating to the teachers' language competence and their access to an appropriate methodology. Brumfit suggests that we can learn much from mother tongue teaching methodologies (see also the articles in Part 2 of this Collection), and he suggests we should produce reasons for *not* adopting the methods of the mother tongue teacher in the second language classroom (an idea reinforced also in Part 3).

Both Freudenstein and Khan take as their starting points the report on the pilot project to teach French in UK primary schools (Burstall *et al.*, 1974). Though completed some years ago, the report still influences opinion on the issue of the early introduction of foreign language learning into public education systems, at least within Europe.

Freudenstein believes the influence of the report has been unduly negative, that society and education systems have developed since the report, and that, with the emergence of a multilingual Europe, needs have changed and become more clearly defined. He writes from the viewpoint of one who is clearly convinced of the benefits of early learning of second and third languages and, rather than questioning policy on the issue, he puts a strong case for identifying problems of implementation and seeking solutions to them.

Case studies in the area of primary-level language learning should be a rich source of information on problems of implementation, though care must be taken not to generalise too freely from one situation to another. Khan's description of some of the 'lessons worth remembering' from the UK French primary project is an example of the value of the case study approach. She identifies a number of useful principles and matters of practice, some of which are also discussed by Freudenstein, which could usefully be fed into any future projects in this area. Among the elements most crucial for the success of any project appear to be continuity of the learning and teaching from primary to secondary level, teachers who are both trained to teach at primary level and confident users of the foreign language concerned, and the necessity for the project to respond to real needs rather than (presumably) political expedience. These issues and the question of an appropriate methodology for primary-level foreign language learning we shall see raised by the other contributors to this volume.

The writers in this section implicitly suggest areas where research is required. Thus the claims of intellectual and mother-tongue improvement, and cultural gains resulting from early foreign language learning need careful evaluation, especially since they may be associated with programmes in particular social and geographical contexts. And one suspects that governments considering allocating scarce resources to primary-level language programmes will be concerned with the utilitarian question of whether there are substantial linguistic gains at this level and whether such gains lead to accelerated learning of foreign languages at higher levels in the educational system.

# Young learners: Young language

## Christopher Brumfit

In recent years British ELT expertise has increasingly addressed itself to the teaching of young learners. However, while it is clear that there have been strong British traditions in areas directly relevant to primary ELT, it is less clear that there is a large body of experienced classroom practitioners to call upon. British people who have spent many years directly teaching the English language to junior age children are relatively rare. For these, we need to turn more to non-native-speaking teachers in overseas countries. It would be disastrous if innovation and development were to come exclusively from people experienced in advising, teacher training, and other support services, or from teaching higher age levels, rather than from those whose main professional experience has been teaching this language at this level of the school system.

All I can hope to offer in this paper is a perspective, based on experience of a number of education systems, and of language teaching theory and practice, at a fairly abstract level. I may thus be able to give a general framework for more detailed examination of specific problems – but the value of such a framework needs to be constantly tested against experience of particular learners in particular education systems, with particular groups of teachers.

An example of the kind of difficulty I am referring to results from asking the fundamental question: Is there any such thing as 'Primary English Language Teaching' in a global sense? Clearly, in many countries there is English language teaching in schools for young age groups. But the key elements in the concept of 'Primary ELT' vary considerably from culture to culture. What we mean by 'childhood' itself is a major culture variable, and the purposes of and needs in language learning also vary. So too do attitudes to authority, to teaching, and to learning in general. Young learners are only just beginning to be socialised into the international world of formal education, mass communications, and mass certification and qualification; as a group they are potentially more differentiated than secondary or adult learners, for they are closer to their varied home cultures, and new to the conformity increasingly imposed across cultural groupings by the school.

Singleton (1989: 242–5), in a discussion of reasons for teaching language at junior levels, suggests a number which do not rely on claims that language is most effectively learnt at that stage. These include arguments about internalisation of the world (including the concept of foreign cultures) at early ages, the need for more instructional time and thus exposure over a language-learning career (Genesee, 1978; Hatch, 1983), and the possibility of early language learning allowing later FL-medium instruction at secondary level (Titone, 1986). These views, and other similar ones, reflect differing expectations of the role of the school, differing degrees of economic support for schooling, different expectations about teacher competence, and a number of other variable cultural factors. Singleton produces a useful checklist of factors of this kind which may be relevant.

(i)     Are the course materials to be used
- commercially produced and aimed at no particular age-group?
- commercially produced and aimed at older learners?
- commercially produced with the generality of younger learners in mind?
- locally produced (whether commercially or not) with local younger learners in mind?
- produced by one particular teacher with one particular class of younger learners in mind?
- some combination of the above?
- principally oriented towards the written language?
- principally oriented towards the spoken language?
- oriented towards both the written and the spoken language?
- dependent on a very restricted range of presentation modes and activity-types?
- flexible and varied in the presentation modes and activity-types employed?
- devoid of or replete with content which reflects learners' interests?

(ii)    Does the teaching personnel consist of
- primary school teachers with only minimal training and interest in the language to be taught?
- primary school teachers with substantial training but little interest in the language to be taught?
- primary school teachers with substantial training and interest in the language to be taught?
- specialists in/native speakers of the language to be taught with only minimal training in respect of primary level teaching?
- specialists in/native speakers of the language to be taught with substantial training in respect of primary level teaching?
- some combination of the above?

(iii)   Is the language to be taught widely regarded in the community as
- of little cultural or vocational value?
- of little cultural value but vocationally valuable?
- of little vocational value but culturally valuable?
- of high cultural and vocational value?
- of little importance either nationally or internationally?
- of little national importance but important internationally?
- of little international importance but important nationally?
- of importance both nationally and internationally?
- representative of a culture which is on the whole congenial?
- representative of a culture which is on the whole uncongenial?

Many of the broader issues raised by Singleton are not within the control of individual teachers, however, and some of them will reflect general social views which education cannot directly change at all. In the rest of this paper, I propose to concentrate on areas which we need to understand if we are to produce satisfactory policies. First, I shall discuss factors directly relating to the age of the learners; second, I shall briefly consider the needs of primary teachers in training; and third, I shall look at some issues of curriculum organisation.

Children are widely perceived to learn second languages more rapidly than adults, and a number of proposals have been made to account for this perception. However, there is still an extensive debate in progress over whether in fact children are better at learning than adults. They may not be better at learning, but may simply have far more favourable opportunities than adults. Young children, after all, are in a permanent learning environment, with parents, friends, and teachers all contributing to their development. Social pressures and personal needs alike strongly push children to learn. It is extremely difficult to determine whether their learning benefits from these external conditions, or from some internal characteristics of the young brain or the young character.

Nonetheless, a number of different proposals have been made, and it may be helpful to distinguish the key elements that scholars have discussed.

One claim is that the maturation process favours early learning of language. The main source of this view is Lenneberg (1967) whose 'critical period' hypothesis suggests that up to about puberty the child's brain is particularly adaptable and capable of acquiring language without apparent effort – and that this adaptability extends to second language when the opportunity is there. When people learn second languages after puberty, it is argued, they use different, and usually more self-conscious, strategies. However, the effect of this on performance, even if it is true, seems to be limited to the ease of acquisition of a foreign accent. There is no strong evidence that any other linguistic features are intrinsically harder to acquire at a more advanced age, and even the claim about accent has been disputed (Christopherson, 1972).

Emotional and affective factors may be seen as the most significant element. Schumann (1975) reviews these, and suggests that children are less likely to be ill-disposed towards new languages or new cultural experiences than adults. If this is indeed the case, we might expect children to be generally better motivated towards learning languages than older learners.

Other commentators have suggested that children have opportunities for integrating their new-language experience with real communication more satisfactorily than adults. Child language, it is suggested, depends more on immediate environment than adult language, and consequently is more fully supported for learning than ordinary adult interaction is (Wagner-Gough & Hatch, 1975).

A fourth factor which suggests that young learners have advantages is the simple one of time. Apart from the fact that an early start allows more total time for learning over a school-life, it is also likely that young learners have more learning time at their disposal than adults, who are surrounded by family and work responsibilities which cut into their learning time.

Harley concludes a survey of the role of age in second language acquisition by commenting that 'although most theorists would agree that there is at least some potential advantage to an early start in childhood, there is little consensus on the precise nature of such an advantage' (Harley, 1986: 22). More recently, Singleton (1989: 137–8) reaches broadly similar conclusions.

What is clear from the discussion so far is that there are no strong reasons in children, or in the normal structure of children's learning, for refusing to teach them second languages. There may, however, be strong reasons which relate to teachers and materials – for there is little justification for exposing learners to large numbers of teachers who are themselves unconfident about their ability to teach and use the language being learnt. In practice, the needs of teachers may be more important than abstract learning principles in achieving success or failure. What kind of support do teachers need?

First, of course, they need the language. A degree of competence is necessary. This may pose problems in some educational traditions, especially where foreign rather than second languages are being learnt. Primary teachers in many educational systems are likely to be less academically orientated than secondary or tertiary teachers, and opportunities for foreign language access will vary considerably from country to country. It is true that (like all language teachers) they need as much competence as possible in the language. But it may be necessary to relate the teachers' second language development closely with teaching methodology for this level.

Secondly, and more crucially, teachers need access to primary teaching methodology. The shift from teaching adults or secondary learners to teaching young children is a radical shift. Small children are charming and exasperating, demanding, exhausting and rewarding all at the same time. The skills necessary for teaching at this level are very different from those needed elsewhere in the education system (though perhaps we should be borrowing some of them more frequently for older pupils). We need to emphasise the role of story (see, e.g. Garvie, this volume), dance, role-play and puppet activity, model-making, and so on, and we shall need to centre much of our teaching on topical rather than formal organisation. Experienced primary teachers will already be familiar with these procedures, but EFL teachers who wish to move from other levels to consider work with young children have a major reorientation to undertake with their expectations of teaching – at least as great a change as for an experienced primary teacher learning a new language.

The key problem for primary EFL teachers at the moment must be the relation between mother tongue practices and EFL practices drawn from higher levels in the educational system. Much of our current theory of language teaching presses us towards naturalistic methods. We have already commented that young learners are held to be successful partly because the language development is closely integrated with their developing thought processes and their communicative needs. If we accept these implications of communicative language teaching ideas, we should at least explore links between mother tongue and foreign language practices.

It happens that in Britain this is a good period to attempt to do this. Practices in British teaching are currently being codified for the National Curriculum, and the views of many advisors on English teaching are available through the report of the Cox Committee (DES, 1988), and the subsequent advice from the National Curriculum Council (NCC, 1989).

These codifications provide a point of reference for considerations of second language work. They are in fact freely available for reproduction without copyright restrictions, and they constitute a starting point for a communicative set of activities, for young learners, which second language learning should run behind. It is at least arguable that many of these capacities could be developed in a second language alongside development of similar capacities in the mother tongue. As a checklist for development of second language curricular strategies, these will have several advantages. First, they will prevent us being too willing to underestimate possible levels of attainment, by linking us to language skills that are encouraged in the mother tongue. Second, they will be, as far as possible, contextualised activities, drawing upon the experience of teachers who have worked with children at this level. Third, none of them is pointless – they will force us to defend departures from these activities as absolutely essential for second language learners, and thus prevent us from simply falling back on the stereotypes of the past, or on the practices devised for older learners. The key challenge I would wish to leave us with, then, is what reasons we can produce for not doing all the things in a second language which are outlined on the next four pages for first language learners.

## Acknowledgement

Singleton's checklist on page 10 is from *Language Acquisition: The Age Factor* and is reproduced with the permission of Multilingual Matters Ltd, Bank House, 8A Hill Road, Clevedon, Avon.

The Attainment Targets in Appendix 1 are from *English in the National Curriculum* and are reproduced with the permission of the Controller of Her Majesty's Stationery Office.

**Appendix 1**

ATTAINMENT TARGET 1: SPEAKING AND LISTENING

Pupils should demonstrate their understanding of the spoken word and the capacity to express themselves effectively in a variety of speaking and listening activities, matching style and response to audience and purpose.

Throughout all these statements of attainment (in AT1) the importance of audibility should be stressed, particularly where 'presentation' is involved.

**Pupils should be able to:**

| Level | *Statements of attainment* | *Example* |
|---|---|---|
| 1 | Participate as a speaker and listener in group activities. | |
| | Respond to instructions given by a teacher. | |
| | Listen attentively, and respond, to stories and poems. | |
| | Participate orally in imaginative play. | After hearing both unfamiliar and familiar nursery rhymes and stories, pupils will begin to memorise them and to use them in imaginative play. |
| 2 | Participate as a speaker and listener in a group engaged in a prescribed task. | In a task in science or technology, for example. |
| | Talk confidently to the teacher; ask and answer questions, listen and respond to increasingly complex instructions. | The context should be one in which the pupil feels certain of having a contribution to make. This should be directly related to the pupil's current learning. |
| | Describe briefly an event to the teacher or another pupil. | The event should be concerned with the pupil's own recent experience. |
| | Listen attentively to stories and poems, and talk about their response. | Pupils talk about the story or poem, reflecting upon the content, and show signs of developing preferences. |

## ATTAINMENT TARGET 2: READING

The development of the ability to read, understand and respond to all types of writing, as well as the development of information-retrieval strategies for the purposes of study.

### Pupils should be able to:

| *Level* | *Statements of attainment* | *Example* |
|---|---|---|
| 1 | Recognise that print carries meaning, both in books and in the everyday world. | In labels, notices, signs. |
|  | Show signs of a developing interest in reading. | By turning to books, readily choosing ones which they would like to hear or read, talking about them, retelling stories they have enjoyed. |
|  | Discuss the content of stories, or relevant aspects of information books. | The pupil should be encouraged to ask and answer relevant questions about what has been heard or read. |
|  | Begin to recognise individual words or letters in familiar contexts. | e.g. 'P' for Parking and the initial letter of their own name. |
| 2 | Demonstrate knowledge of the alphabet and its application. | In order to use word books, dictionaries, and reference books effectively. |
|  | Use a combination of picture cues, sight cues, vocabulary, phonic and context cues in reading. | When attempting an unfamiliar text chosen by the pupil. |
|  | Describe what has happened in a story and predict what will happen next. | In discussion with other pupils, adults, or the teacher. |
|  | Read with increasing independence, confidence, fluency, accuracy and understanding a range of material. | These should include stories, poems, information books and visual texts. |

| Level | Statements of attainment | Example |
|---|---|---|
| 2 *(continued)* | Listen and respond to stories and poems, expressing opinions informed by what has been read. | This includes being engrossed in a book selected by themselves, and listening with enjoyment to stories and poems. In reading, children will be developing an understanding of how characters feel, as well as their motives and a response to the ending and the way it was written. |
| | Read accurately straight-forward signs, labels and notices. | On out of school visits; in the home-play corner, class shop or another dramatic play setting. |

### ATTAINMENT TARGET 3: WRITING

A growing ability to construct and convey meaning in written language matching style to audience and purpose.

**Pupils should be able to:**

| Level | Statements of attainment | Example |
|---|---|---|
| 1 | Use pictures, symbols or isolated letters, words or phrases to communicate meaning. | |
| 2 | Produce independently short pieces of writing using complete sentences, some demarcated with capital letters and full stops or question marks. | |
| | Write stories showing an understanding of the rudiments of story structure by establishing an opening, characters and one or more events. | |
| | Structure sequences of real or imagined events coherently in chronological accounts. | |
| | Produce simple non-chronological writing. | A description of a person, or thinking about an intended classroom activity. |

ATTAINMENT TARGET 4: SPELLING

**Pupils should be able to:**

| *Level* | *Statements of attainment* |
|---|---|
| 1 | Begin to show an understanding of the difference between drawing and writing, and between numbers and letters. |
| | Write some letter shapes in response to sounds and letter names. |
| | Use single letters or pairs of letters to represent whole words or parts of words. |
| 2 | Produce recognisable (though not necessarily always correct) spelling of a range of common words. |
| | Know that spelling has patterns, and begin to apply that knowledge in order to attempt the spelling of a wider range of words. |
| | Spell correctly words in regular use in their own writing which observe common patterns. |

ATTAINMENT TARGET 5: HANDWRITING

| *Level* | *Statements of attainment* |
|---|---|
| 1 | Begin to form letters with some control over the size, shape and/or orientation of letters or lines of writing. |
| 2 | Produce properly oriented, legible and distinctive upper and lower case letters in one style (e.g. printed). |
| | Use upper and lower case letters consistently (i.e. not randomly mixed within words). |

# *Issues and problems in primary education*

## Reinhold Freudenstein

In 1974, early foreign language learning suffered a severe setback when the results of a British experiment on teaching French at primary level were made available (Burstall *et al.*, 1974). The study simply stressed the fact that a later start in foreign language learning produced certain results in a shorter period of time, which is also true for many other subjects taught at school. The study neither indicated nor implied that there are negative consequences arising from early foreign language learning, and yet it was repeatedly used as proof that teaching foreign languages to young children was more or less a waste of time. In 1974, both the profession and society were obviously not prepared for changes to language programmes in the educational system.

In view of the language needs of a multilingual European society, we should look at the issues again, identify the problems and seek solutions if we are to introduce language learning activities as a normal option during the first four years of formal education.

### ■ Advantages of early foreign language learning

The following advantages have been claimed from research carried out in connection with foreign language teaching at primary level. They are also drawn from personal observation.

#### *Intellectual improvement*

Children who learn a foreign language at an early age tend to be superior to their monolingual peers in verbal and non-verbal behaviour. Intellectually, a child's experience with two language systems seems to give him or her greater mental flexibility, superiority in concept formation and a more diversified set of mental abilities.

#### *Mother-tongue improvement*

Children who start learning a foreign language early in life can understand their native language system better; they become conscious of the existence of language as a phenomenon. It is therefore false to argue negatively that learning a foreign language at primary level interferes with the development of the mother-tongue or even interrupts its acquisition. The basic development of one's mother-tongue comes to an end by the age of four or five. So there should not be any obstructing influence from other languages at primary level. There is a lot of evidence in favour of this argument from many bi- and multilingual children all over the world who do not suffer as a result of knowing and using several languages effectively in their everyday communication.

#### *Cultural gains*

Children who speak foreign languages tend to have a wider cultural outlook than monolingual children who often believe that their own culture and customs are the only ones that matter. Children may be safely exposed to other languages and cultures while still quite young, even before they have identified with their first language and culture. The introduction of a foreign idiom into the child's world helps him or her to develop tolerance towards people who are different and, in the long run, contributes to mutual understanding between individuals and nations. It must be noted, however, that positive cultural values can only result from favourable teaching situations leading to successful learning, e.g. small learning groups, suitable teaching aids, appropriate methodological approaches and properly trained teachers. If these conditions cannot be met, early foreign language teaching might easily be connected with negative experiences in a child's mind, and produce unfavourable attitudes towards another culture. Every effort should be made to arrange for teaching and learning situations in which the foreign language can be discovered in such a way that only positive attitudes can result from, and be connected with it.

The advantages of early language learning with regard to cultural gains show that conventional objections to early foreign language teaching can no longer be accepted as valid. Teaching foreign languages to children at primary level can support the growth of individual qualities of character and it plays an important part in the development of the intellect. There is evidence to support the view that the process of learning other languages alongside the mother-tongue must start at an early age if multilingualism is to be achieved.

## ■ Problems connected with an early start

Rather than continue to reproduce old-fashioned, obsolete prejudices about early foreign language learning, it would be more constructive to concentrate on those problems connected with foreign language learning which have not yet been satisfactorily solved and therefore need further clarification. The following questions and issues now need to be tackled at local, national and international levels, in order to achieve reliable results within a reasonably short period of time.

### *The problem of continuity*

Although it is true that learning a foreign language at primary level is in itself a worthwhile individual educational experience, many early language teaching projects have been discontinued in the past because of inadequate links between language learning in primary schools and in institutions of secondary education. After two or three years of learning a foreign language at primary level children had to start all over again with the same language when they moved to a secondary school. Their motivation and interest in language learning in general often declined in consequence. This lack of continuity also discouraged administrators from pursuing projects in early foreign language teaching. In addition, teachers at secondary level are, as a rule, not familiar with teaching techniques at primary level; they often have a sense that the approach to foreign language instruction which they use with older children is the only effective way to success, and they have received no guidance, either from empirical research or from their own training, with regard to ways of handling the language knowledge which children have previously acquired. It is essential, therefore, to find a way of solving the problem of continuity. It should also be established how early language learning can remain a positive and gainful experience, even if there is no immediate continuation of language learning or of learning the same language as children change schools. Finally, new approaches to initial teacher training are necessary in order to enable foreign language teachers to be more flexible in different teaching situations; future foreign language teachers must be in a position to instruct young children, as well as older pupils and adults.

## *The question of the number of languages*

The experience of Luxembourg shows that it is not unrealistic to introduce more than one foreign language to children at primary level. In Luxembourg, German is offered from Year 1, French from Year 3. The Waldorf school system is an example of two foreign languages (English and French) being offered at the same time to all children from Year 1 onwards. There are countries outside Europe where it is the norm that children have command of two or three languages (as well as their mother-tongue) by the age of ten. On the basis of these models, we need to know what the educational advantages and disadvantages are with regard to the number of languages to be learned by children in the European context. A future Europe requires multilingual citizens; language learning must therefore start as early as possible if it is not to be restricted to only one foreign language.

Finally the introduction of foreign language learning at primary school can also be regarded as a major contribution to a diversified language programme offered during the years of compulsory education. Given due regard for local conditions, an early start need not be restricted to the major languages, and it provides time and opportunity to learn other languages later.

## *Language awareness before language learning*

We should try to establish new models of language learning which could help to overcome the current inadequacies of early language instruction. There are programmes in the United Kingdom which aim to introduce children to several cultures and languages (regional and national dialects, community or foreign languages) at the same time; they try to promote a positive attitude towards languages in general. It might well be that various forms of this kind of 'language awareness' could be the best way of preparing pupils for a multilingual society. If children first learn to understand new values connected with languages spoken in their country (local dialects, the language of immigrants, migrant workers) they will probably be well equipped to choose and learn a foreign language, and so be in a better position later on, when they want to, or have to, speak other languages for professional or private purposes.

## *Language studies in the primary curriculum*

One of the strong objections to early foreign language teaching concerns the risk of overloading the curriculum of primary schools. In projects in the past foreign languages have simply been added to the regular timetable and have thus intensified the feeling that foreign language learning is an additional, time-consuming extra at the expense of free time. We need to know if there are other and better ways of integrating foreign languages in the primary school curriculum. There is a wide spectrum of possibilities: from ten-to-fifteen-minute modules daily to instruction in school subjects, such as Music or Physical Education, through the medium of the foreign language (partial immersion).

## *Language learning at pre-school level*

Research projects of a practical kind need to be conducted to discover if pre-school foreign language learning can prepare and support language instruction at primary level. An early contact with several languages might be the best means of paving the way for multilingual instruction at a later stage. Research in this field should concentrate primarily on two questions:

1  What educational benefits are there for the individual learner?
2  Can monolingualism be overcome in a natural way in situations which are meaningful to children?

In spite of a number of unsolved questions, foreign language learning activities at primary level provide an educational setting in which children can best be prepared for the multicultural challenges of the future.

# *Lessons worth remembering – from primary French in Britain*

## Julia Khan

A pilot scheme for the teaching of French in primary schools was launched in Britain in 1964. Ten years later a report entitled *Primary French in the Balance* (Burstall *et al.*, 1974) effectively halted the scheme.

The sequence of events was as follows. In March 1963 the British Minister of Education (then Edward Boyle) announced the launching of a scheme within which the Nuffield Foundation and the Ministry of Education would co-operate to develop modern language studies as a new venture in junior schools. The Ministry would select areas and schools for the pilot scheme. Local education authorities were invited to volunteer to take part. About 80 volunteered – thirteen were chosen to cover a range of types of school and area. In all, 125 schools were to participate, involving about 6000 children. In September 1964, all eight-year olds in the pilot schools began the first year of their French course. The National Foundation for Educational Research (NFER) and Her Majesty's Inspectorate (HMI) were to evaluate the children's achievement over the following five years.

Let us briefly put these facts into context. The early sixties were a time of optimism and expansion in education. Euro-consciousness was growing. The Annan Committee Report on The Teaching of Russian had drawn attention to the potential benefit for language learning in Britain if 'the regular teaching of a first modern language were started in good conditions and by the right methods in primary schools' (quoted in Schools Council, 1966, p.1). Funding was available – the Nuffield Foundation was sponsoring other educational initiatives and there had been successful preliminary initiatives.

The project was centrally co-ordinated. It was related to what seemed like relevant research – investigations into the language of eight-, nine-, and ten-year old children. It was supported by specially designed materials – the *En Avant* scheme (E J Arnold). The project received advice/consultancy from sound sources and teacher-training programmes were mounted. The NFER produced three reports, *French from Eight* (1968), *French in the Primary School* (1970), and *Primary French in the Balance* (1974).

The project was planned as a pilot project and the five basic questions that were intended to be answered by the research and the project were:

1  Is any substantial gain in mastery of a foreign language achieved by beginning to teach it at eight instead of eleven?
2  Do other aspects of education and general intellectual development gain or suffer from the introduction of a foreign language in the primary school?
3  What are the organisational, teaching and other problems posed by such an experiment?
4  Are there levels of ability below which the teaching of a foreign language is of dubious value?
5  What methods, incentives and motivations are most effective in fostering learning of a foreign language? (Schools Council, 1966, p.3)

There had been few carefully designed longitudinal studies of the factors affecting the acquisition of a foreign language during the early school years.

This was, therefore, a splendid research opportunity.

In the final report (Burstall *et al.*, 1974) it was reported after extensive testing that other aspects of children's educational development had neither gained nor suffered at primary level but that at secondary level there was 'more loss than profit' (p.242), largely because of early disenchantment with foreign language learning. There was no clear-cut conclusion about levels of ability below which the experience had been of little benefit but for some children, it was reported that a sense of failure had developed and for them, the learning of French was 'a profitless experience' (p.243). Discussion of the organisational and teaching problems within the project was extensive, as was discussion of methods and motivation, and these will be explored in this article. The final conclusion, however, was that no greater mastery was achieved by starting at eight rather than eleven and that therefore the spending of resources was not easily justified. The pilot scheme appeared to have proved that it was not worth extending the practice.

So what went wrong? The conclusions appeared to imply that factors intrinsic to primary-level foreign language teaching made the continuation ill-advised. Yet everyone was aware that excellent reasons for starting foreign language learning early were still valid – that longer exposure should mean more achievement, that young children's capacity for developing accurate pronunciation does not endure, that broadening horizons is educationally desirable. It is important, too, to recognise that some very effective work had taken place within the project. This was acknowledged by the inspectors who contributed to the report and was recognised by many teachers and teacher trainers at classroom level. Reflection at this distance makes it possible to understand the situation more fully, however. The context of the project was British but the lessons that can be learned have broader implications, particularly within the fields of methodology, teacher training and management.

## ■ Methodology and materials

The *En Avant* materials – five volumes – to provide for three years in primary school and two at subsequent secondary school, were developed strictly in accordance with the principles of the then popular audio-visual approach. The principle of oral language having to come first was unquestioned – two years of the materials limit themselves exclusively to oral work; a little exposure to written text is permitted in the third year.

> The approach to the language in the Nuffield course is predominantly oral, the language being regarded first and foremost as a means of communication ... Research has been carried out to ensure that the material is linguistically sound and the greatest care is taken to ensure maximum authenticity e.g. in the use of French speakers in the recordings on the tape. (Schools Council, 1966, pp. 6–7)

Materials included flannelgraph figures, flash cards, wallcharts, tapes, teacher's book, film strips, slides, Stage 2 workbooks and readers. The tape-recorder was of central importance for the presentation of new material and for extensive repetition and drilling exercises.

In teacher-training courses preparing teachers to use materials, principles were clearly laid down:

> Emphasis throughout was placed on the vital importance of spoken French and the need for daily practice; reading and writing must wait until the child has acquired the power of listening and repeating the various speech patterns so that they were fixed in his memory and associated directly with situations and ideas which had meaning and interest for him. Success in this approach depended on the teacher's skill in introducing a limited vocabulary and giving the children the opportunity of using the same restricted material in a variety of different ways ... The child had to acquire an instinctive response to a linguistic stimulus ... The sequence of learning – listen, repeat, see, write – must be maintained; and when the printed word was ultimately introduced, the starting point must always be to proceed from familiar material. (Schools Council, 1966, p.24)

Guidelines were rigorous: start at age eight, allow no errors for fear of bad habits, provide extensive repetition, use only French in the classroom, limit input to what is reproducible, give little and often, always use visual support, no room for reading and writing in the first two years.

The need for classroom language was recognised if French was to be used all the time. Top of the list in the teacher's manual came significant phrases: *Ecoute le magnétophone. Branche le magnétophone. Appuie sur le bouton. Tire les rideaux. Ne parle pas anglais. Fais-moi une phrase complète. Répète.* (Listen to the tape-recorder. Plug in the tape-recorder. Press the switch. Pull the curtains. Don't speak English. Give me a whole sentence. Repeat.)

Attractive visual materials played an important role. Dialogues, songs, games, situations were key features. The *En Avant* materials were used by some 80 per cent of the schools in the pilot scheme. It was, though, characteristic of the whole period that many primary schools other than the pilot schools chose to start offering French as part of their programme. Some bought the *En Avant* materials; others started from a far less well resourced basis.

Concern was voiced in the early stages that language learning might have a harmful effect upon the child-centred approach to primary education favoured by most: 'It was suggested by some that the repetitive nature of language learning especially in the early stage might prove inconsistent with the freer, "discovery" methods of learning in other areas of the curriculum ...' (Schools Council, 1966, p.5).

The organisers of the project never really questioned the basis of audio-visual methodology beforehand. The verdict of *Primary French in the Balance* as regards methodology was, however:

> No single method is equally appropriate for all pupils ... There are however certain aspects of learning French which children of all levels of achievement tend to reject, such as the enforced passivity, repetition and incomprehension associated with the use of the tape-recorder and the practice of reading French aloud, which for most children acts as a source of embarrassment and a barrier to understanding. (Burstall *et al.*, 1974, p.244)

Children's own responses to questionnaires had shown this (after three years):

> Even those who like French report that they do not always understand what they are saying when they speak in French but are simply repeating meaningless sounds. This is true of 68 per cent of the sample: 62 per cent of those who like French and 75 per cent of those who do not like French ... Many children report that they find particular difficulty in understanding spoken French when they hear it on the tape-recorder. Over 75 per cent of the total sample agree that it is more difficult to understand the tape-recorder than their teacher. This is equally true of those who like French and those who dislike French: 'French is very boring when you have to listen to the tape-recorder over and over again. It is much easier to learn when your teacher says it through for you'; 'People say that French is boring, but I think it is the tape-recorder that is boring ...' (Burstall, 1970, p.52)

Ironically, however, (given all the emphasis on few words) secondary school teachers subsequently complained:

> It would appear that there was not enough attention paid to mistakes in pronunciation at the primary stage, so that certain errors (e.g. confusion of le/la, un/une, grand/grande) did persist. Also the fact that children did understand the gist of sentences may have led to inattention to component words so that a rough estimate was too easily accepted in written work. The children are still easily satisfied with superficial understanding; they do not ask many questions about words. (Burstall, 1970, p.114)

Research also showed that greatest achievement was by children taught by teachers well grounded in primary practice.

Reflection upon experience and upon the report can give rise to a number of observations. First, notions about communication and authentic language were over-simplified. It was assumed that provided there was a lot of emphasis on production of oral language, children's communicative skills were being developed. The need for children to experience using the language for communication was not fully understood. Authenticity was associated largely with the voices heard on the tapes. Secondly, the 'minimalist' approach of providing children with very little input clearly squandered the learning resources of the young. Those teachers whose own skills were not great often did not have the confidence or ability to adapt the materials. Thirdly, the tape-recorder can obviously be as much of a danger as a help. Using it as the major means of presenting or practising new language is unsatisfactory. Of course, good audio tape resources are a great asset but the tape-recorder can distance and de-personalise the language and make practice activities impossibly mechanical. This can be particularly inappropriate for the young learner. Again, it was the teacher who lacked confidence or skill who was most inclined to keep rigidly to the prescribed format and rely heavily on the tape-recorder. Finally, it will often be secondary schools who judge the effectiveness of primary school teaching. If there is a significant mismatch between the way the two sectors perceive their objectives, this can be damaging to primary school achievements.

## ■ Teacher training

Teacher training for the pilot scheme was extensive. Colleges of education offered French as main and subsidiary subjects on B.Ed courses.[1] Local authorities and training institutions offered courses. It was recognised that teacher supply could be a problem and it is interesting to look at how that was approached in the short term.

A policy decision was made that 'it was reasonable to suppose from the outset that, given adequate additional training both in French and in up-to-date methods, the average primary school teacher whose qualifications in French might be limited to a pass at 'O' level,[2] acquired perhaps some years ago, and whose fluency in the language was likely, to start with, to be limited, would be able to teach the early stages well' (Schools Council, 1966, p.3). Statistics provided in research reports show that such teachers formed the biggest group. Language upgrading courses were 'organised around a language laboratory' and ranged from 25–90 hours (ibid., 1966, p.9).

In schools trying to follow the model of the pilot schools, this often meant that if a head teacher wanted to introduce French into his school, he sought a teacher with 'O' level French, not always the most willing or confident. Certainly local training courses received a wide range of ability. Alternatively, a locally-based French national might be found.

To respond to the needs of inexperienced teachers, *En Avant* led the teacher by the hand. Every exercise is prescribed and described. Of course one of the problems was that many teachers with 'O' level had done little or no talking in their own French course at school, but had been mainly involved in writing and translating.

In the early sixties, there was a very large increase in the number of students who were recruited on to teacher-training first degree courses to become French specialists, but recruitment was not easy. These four-year courses, run by Colleges of Education, offered a balance of academic and professional input, developing trainees' skills in French and their teaching skills alongside each other. A sound principle in such courses is that methods used for the students' own academic development must exemplify good professional practice and, insofar as is appropriate, adhere to principles that it is hoped trainees will embrace in their teaching. Emphasis on development of oral skills would, for example, be appropriate in this case. But Colleges of Education had to have their courses approved and validated externally, for example by universities. Gaining approval for the idea of giving weighting in assessment for oral performance was sometimes seen as academically suspect. The importance of translation as a means of developing language skills was not easily questioned. Again we see that traditions at one level can make innovation difficult at another level.

Of course, teaching practice time provided contact with the target situation. Introducing other tutors in a training institution to the notion of supervising students who might be teaching some French required careful planning. A document issued to such tutors gives insight into methods proposed in training:

> The teaching of French will often appear rather 'formal', but this is almost inevitable. Independent and group work are very difficult to arrange in French. Either they depend on the use of the written language at too early a stage or they involve children in using the oral language independently before they are equipped to do so ... It is essential, in the early stages that the material should be 'audio-visual', i.e. it should be designed to permit in the mind of the child immediate and unambiguous association of concept and language ... The sequence which is generally accepted is the following: 1. Listen – understand; 2. Imitate – speak independently; 3. Read known material; 4. Write – copying only; 5. Read unseen material; 6. Write independently. Tutors will very rarely find a class involved in work beyond stage 2 of the above sequence. (Coventry College of Education, 1967)

What did the NFER reports say about the pilot scheme which could have bearing upon this whole area of teacher training? Of central importance was the observation from the HMI who monitored the scheme that 'no feature of the teaching situation was considered as important a factor in the development of proficiency in French (amongst the children) as the teacher's skill in the use of primary teaching methods. Such skill was felt to outweigh even linguistic competence as a determinant of successful French teaching at the primary level' (Burstall, 1970, p.83). Inadequate teaching was seen as deriving not from the French teacher's lack of linguistic ability but rather from lack of experience as a primary teacher or lack of specific training for primary teaching. 'Poor' teachers were described as having 'much to learn about technique' and 'little idea about oral methods', showing 'lack of appreciation of the children's difficulties' and allowing pupils 'little scope for using their initiative'. To sum up, the worst threats to children's interests derived from inexperienced teachers unused to oral approaches, from teachers who were good French speakers but who were unfamiliar with primary methods, from teachers who were poor French speakers but who had reasonable teaching methods, from teachers who were over-active and allowed the children no initiative and from situations where there were very frequent changes of staff (ibid., p.82).

These points can provide timely reminders irrespective of teaching approaches.

## ■ Management

Two dimensions of management will be considered here. The primary French project will be looked at as an example of an educational innovation and, within that context, the schools will be discussed. We may start from the second focus, for the secondary schools were really the source of the final verdict that there was no overall gain in mastery as a result of starting at eight rather than eleven. Although there was no loss in overall achievement in French, the pilot scheme was deemed to have proved the whole idea pointless.

The scheme was mounted in the expectation and hope that the long-term effect in the secondary schools would be that more children would do a second foreign language. Another key issue at the time was the question of whether one could usefully extend foreign language teaching to pupils of all ability levels.

The extension of Spanish, Russian and German occurred to some extent. Where it did happen, it was not acknowledged to be a result of primary French.

What is obvious in the research reports is the readiness of many secondary schools to see the project as not useful. Many acknowledged that oral standards were higher amongst pilot scheme pupils, but balanced the verdict by saying that writing skills were actually worse. The sixties were still the days of segregated-by-ability schooling[3] in many places, and grammar schools, on the whole, did not favour primary French. Secondary modern schools did, and so did comprehensive schools where they were in operation.

However, advantages were often lost because of organisational factors. The pilot scheme tried to organise experimental schools so that secondary schools would recruit children with similar backgrounds. There had, however, been a wide range of local initiatives in primary schools that were not officially involved in the pilot project but where the headteacher perhaps wished pupils to be able to take part in what seemed like an exciting new area of curriculum development. A great many primary schools had, therefore, introduced the teaching of some French. As a result, it often happened that secondary schools found themselves recruiting mixed groups: three years of good French, three years of mediocre, two years of good or mediocre French, one year of experience or none at all. The difficulty of then providing for students' needs was too great. The temptation, solution perhaps, was simply to start again. And so, often, this was the verdict in the final report – there was more loss than profit to the secondary schools because they could not accommodate the achievements of the children, and so suffered their subsequent disappointments. The French department could, with many children, no longer benefit from the fact that French had novelty value.

Furthermore, the French exams the children were to take remained unchanged. They would be the same for children who had done eight years or five years of French. If secondary schools were still working to the same leaving certificate syllabuses and exams, there was little incentive to change methods and materials.

These problems were recognised early on – but at local level little was done or could be done.

Attempts were made to carry over materials: *En Avant* had two volumes for the first two years of secondary school. But they were less used than the traditional beginners' books because they were not relevant for all children.

As an exercise in innovation, therefore, (to address the broader question) the project could claim to have been extremely well designed in that objectives were clearly defined, training resources were carefully prepared and supplied, materials were specifically designed for its implementation and monitoring was close and meticulous. But on other counts, problems were perhaps inevitable. First, not all of those who would be significantly affected were represented in the planning. The secondary schools had little say except at the evaluation stage. Even the primary teachers were recruited or trained for the scheme. In other words, the scheme was not teacher-led and therefore ran the risk of being unwelcome.

The innovation was not really needs-led either. Its chances of being perceived as successful would have been greater if French had been needed in the primary school and the effectiveness of pupils' learning could have been measured in relation to that need. As it was, it was an exciting new idea without a very clear practical objective.

Overall, a number of factors are worth highlighting:

1 Difficulties arose because the pilot scheme expanded too quickly, leading to the problem of teacher supply and local management.
2 A project should respond to a perceived or real need.
3 The support of all those affected has to be engaged.
4 Primary school efforts will often be judged by secondary schools. Their instruments of evaluation may not always be well adjusted to do so.
5 If one sector of a system changes, other sectors must accommodate that change.
6 Teachers must be competent enough linguistically and professionally to be able to deviate from the prescribed book. A strongly prescriptive course can be stifling. The effects of using teachers who lack confidence and competence will be to make them over-dependent on and vulnerable to a prescriptive course book.
7 Teachers of young learners must have a primary orientation.
8 So far as methods are concerned, a rich diet, a varied diet, and no dogma, are recommended.

## Acknowledgement

Extracts in this paper are reproduced from *French in the Primary School*, Schools Council, with the permission of the Controller of Her Majesty's Stationery Office, and from *Primary French in the Balance*, Burstal *et al.*, with the permission of NFER–NELSON Publishing Co. Ltd.

## Notes

1 First degree undergraduate courses.
2 'O' level was a British school leaving examination, generally at age sixteen.
3 Before the introduction of comprehensive, non-selective secondary schooling in Britain, pupils were selected at age eleven either for a grammar school, if they passed the exam, or for a secondary modern school if they did not.

# *Part 2*
# Teaching: influences and ideas

## *Introduction*

The first two papers in Part 2 present fascinating points of comparison between the different 'worlds' of English language teaching – as a foreign language (FL), as a second language (SL), and as a mother-tongue (MT). They present personal experience, and suggest ways in which each 'world' can learn from the others, and find deeper understanding of itself. Machura, who works with EFL learners in Poland, describes her experience of the way native-speakers of English are taught in Britain. She points out how FL teachers can be helped by awareness of young native-speakers' problems in developing skills such as writing. The awareness can be a valuable means of helping FL teachers have realisable expectations about what their FL learners can achieve. Such comparisons can also help FL teachers see more value in their own traditions, and so gain more confidence in what they do. Machura's paper also gives an observer's insight into 'project teaching' in action, giving clear examples of what it can mean in a MT context. Scott's paper also presents personal experience – of 'collaborative' teaching in British schools with multilingual pupils. Scott shows ways in which SL-support and mainstream teachers can work together to plan and implement projects in the classroom, to benefit both mother-tongue and second-language speakers of English. However, Scott puts language support programmes in Britain into their political and wider educational contexts, and reminds us of the power of these on both teachers and children. The two papers raise the question of how methods developed in one 'world' can be applicable in others. They do not claim to provide answers, but offer examples of one direction, that of increasing understanding of ways of making language *meaningful* for young learners.

Marsden and Garvie's papers suggest two practical approaches to teaching. Marsden presents six categories of use of cartoon story video, ranging from activities to support comprehension to using the characters as attractive models of language for children to mimic. TV and video are familiar aspects of children's life in many parts of the world, and cartoon stories can exploit that familiarity, and bring a wholly meaningful context of language use into the classroom. What is interesting here, however, is that the video is using *story*, which, as Garvie argues, is one of our most salient ways of making sense. Garvie seeks to expand the teacher's repertoire of techniques for story-exploitation and presents many ideas of what teachers can do. She argues for the power of story to create learner-involvement in learning. Both papers can be seen to highlight the importance of presenting young learners with language which they can relate to their knowledge of human intention and motive. Perhaps story is, in this way, particularly supportive of children's sense-making abilities.

Dunn's paper suggests that what goes on in classrooms can be very greatly helped by enlisting parents as language support persons at home. Drawing on ideas used in home support schemes in Britain, she suggests how parents can be involved in paired reading or listening work with young children. The close attention the child receives from the parent can help in many psychologically important ways; particularly as the new language is given status in the home. In the paper we again have the suggestion of the wider applicability of an idea from a specific language teaching world. While each teacher has to weigh the possibilities in his/her own context, it is surely worth raising the idea of extending the child's active exposure to English to the home.

# British school English and foreign learner's English – two different worlds?

## Ludmila Machura

### ■ Introduction

When, at my first IATEFL Conference in 1987, I noticed talks on ESL or even primary school teaching in the UK, I discarded them as totally irrelevant to my experience and needs. EFL, I believed, had its specific rules and requirements, marked by learners' ultimate goals (of which bilingualism was the least essential). It had its time constraints, mother-tongue influences and, in politically and economically isolated countries of Eastern Europe, limited availability of materials and native-speakers. However, only two years later I found myself investigating British education not solely for academic interest but in the hope of adopting ideas, techniques and materials to give EFL teaching in Poland a wider scope.

Why this drastic change? There have been several reasons. Firstly, recent months have witnessed a sudden political and cultural opening and subsequent demand for more profound contacts and understanding. This resulted in growing efforts to establish not only new language courses encompassing primary school learners but language schools with English used as a medium of instruction – a trend, I understand, fairly common all over Europe.

Secondly, educators have become aware of the increasing number of bilingual children who, after many years abroad, are coming back to Poland. On the one hand they need understanding of their foreign experiences and support in adjusting to the new environment. On the other hand, these children, once outside the English-speaking context, quickly lose the acquired competence and need help to keep up the language. So far, however, no institution or courses have been prepared to cater for these particular needs.

Thirdly, British education is, to most students and teachers of English, a dry, few-page description of the system in *Britain Today* or any such book on life and institutions. Being in Britain I was determined to learn more about how this system works. I also hoped that involvement with schools would help me understand the somewhat ambiguous terms which have marred the last few years in TEFL (also in teaching young learners). It might show me what lies behind such catchwords as: 'task-and-topic based', 'holistic', 'experiential', 'integrated', 'cross-curricular', 'language for life', 'project', and 'primary school philosophy'.

And last, but most directly responsible for my interest, was the fact that I was bound to find out more about schools due to my daughter. She was going through her first week at school when she asked me to help her with the homework – writing a letter from the king of Portugal to Christopher Columbus refusing to finance his voyage. It was then that I became genuinely interested in the type of work school children do. The letter to

Columbus sounded like a follow-up to a role-play or a writing task from any EFL course book and it intrigued me as to which subject the children were studying. As it later turned out, it was Geography.

The longer I thought about the two worlds, the more they looked like two ends of a Christmas cracker (see Fig. 1), with the middle part containing some surprise. Will the content turn out to be useless rubbish or of some value, once the cracker is pulled apart? Will there be any common ground of comparison, any inspiring resemblances? To seek answers, I spent nearly thirty hours of lesson observation in primary and secondary schools in Glasgow. The results of my project will be discussed below when the two educational systems (Scottish and Polish), the teaching techniques, materials and samples of children's writings will be juxtaposed. However, there is no single answer to the question posed in the title. The conclusions will be open to individual interpretations as each teacher draws on his/her own experience and needs.

Fig.1

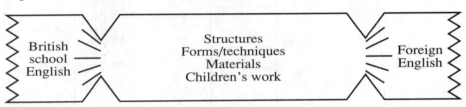

British school English | Structures Forms/techniques Materials Children's work | Foreign English

## ■ Structure

The two systems are compared in Fig. 2 by pupils' age and by the number of years children spend in each school. Asterisks mark the classes I visited. Dots stand for project or task-based teaching techniques which are used in both systems, but apparently not to the same extent and not in the same places.

Children in Scotland begin school at the age of four or five, complete seven years of primary education, then enter secondary schools when they are eleven or twelve and study there for four to six years. By the time they go to university, they can be as young as seventeen.

In Poland children have a one-year preparatory course during the kindergarden stage and then begin school at seven. After eight years of primary, and four years of secondary school they enter universities at the age of nineteen to study for a further five years.

This numerical comparison shows that Polish children are late beginners and enter professional life much later than Scottish youth. This may result either in their greater maturity or, on the contrary, in a lack of intellectual and practical independence.

Fig. 2

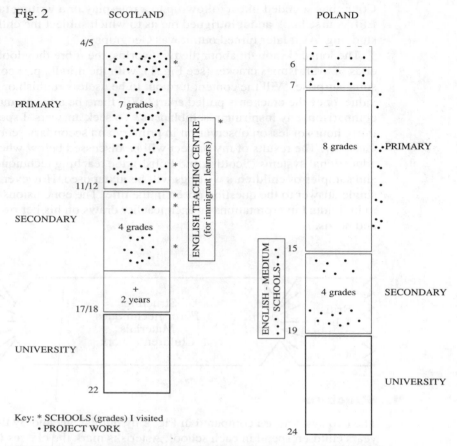

SCOTLAND                 POLAND

Key: * SCHOOLS (grades) I visited
• PROJECT WORK

## ■ Forms of work – projects and task-based activities

### *Glasgow*

I sought direct experience of a mainstream school and visited a primary school in a middle-class suburban district of Glasgow. Primary II was buzzing with activities and bright colours. The thirty children were busy writing in their workbooks, doing maths, making models, reading with the teacher, playing shop, working at the computer. The class was divided into smaller groups, each having a clearly outlined programme of activities for the day. The tasks were specified on the board with symbols, colours and pictures which were known to the children. The teacher was the ultimate controller and supervisor but the children knew their timetable and were made responsible for observing it. This type of work organisation kept all the children busy, involved and stimulated. It varied the tasks and made use of the available utilities and resources to the full.

The Primary VII class I visited next had been involved in an enormous computer-software-supported project on whales developed by Jordanhill College of Education. What I saw when I entered the class (or rather some kind of aquarium), were hundreds of sea birds and fish, a life-size model of an albatross, sailing boats, hunting ships, icebergs and numerous children's writings – poems, captain's log books, news reports written on the word processor, etc. The amount and variety of work, the result of a full term's project, was bewildering. The project relied on a variety of sources and background materials, including reference books, but also literature and music. It generated a lot of language and information, such as on mammals and fish, on wing spans of sea birds and force of winds, on ship loading and whale hunting, etc. It also developed the pupils' independence, ability to plan, co-operate and work together towards common goals.

Project-based activities which require integrated learning constitute the core of the primary school curriculum, or 'philosophy' – as I heard the term used for the first time. However, this form of work is also continued in the early years of secondary schools in Britain, this time more in specialist subjects such as English, Environmental Studies and Science. In English, projects may be focused around reading chosen books and developed into content areas, for example Space Hostages, the Wild West, Holiday Camp, etc. The topics encompass a great variety of language work such as writing stories, formal reports, letters, plays, acting out scenes, conducting interviews and discussions, as well as art work such as drawing and making models of towns.

### Poland

The early years of kindergarten education are based on activities and games (see the density of dots in Fig. 2). However, the moment children enter school at seven, they enter the world of discipline, neat rows of desks, almost bare walls, and the world of rote learning and high requirements. Continental schools are in most cases, as Margaret Donaldson (1978) said, rigid places where children are made anxious by the fear of failure.

English lessons, however, may in some sense be exceptional. On the one hand, many courses are run outside the state system on a voluntary basis (see the dots outside the mainstream school box) and therefore leave greater scope for enjoyment and variety. On the other hand, teaching may be based on varied, non-Polish materials which call for different approaches and forms of work. Private courses of English are offered from very early years of kindergarten and continue into adult education. In the meantime, those primary schools which can find language teachers introduce English lessons in class VII, at thirteen. Teaching is based on the school book *English is Fun* and is still far from being task or project oriented.

### ■ Materials

Due to the lack of appropriate EFL children's materials at my disposal, I compared Scottish school books and EFL materials used at secondary level.

Looking at the covers only, one can mistake *Starting Science* (a school book for the second year of secondary school) for the widely known *Streamline English* – a very popular EFL coursebook. Both are published by OUP, have identical graphics, lay-out, task-oriented and richly illustrated content material. Similar resemblances in format and task types can be found in other British books.

By contrast, an English coursebook for twelve-year old beginners, *English is Fun*, published in Poland in 1982, strikes one by its small, incomprehensible drawings, situational approach and Polish instructions to the grammatical exercises which use terms such as 'adverbials of time'.

Materials for project work in British schools are often organised around themes and come in packs, folders or as checklists. This is exactly what foreign teachers, who work along topic-based syllabuses, have been asking for. They want loose sheets of texts, pictures, diagrams, etc., which can be easily collected, edited, re-shuffled and kept in topic files, rather than sets of coursebooks which are usually very expensive, need adapting and are seldom used from cover to cover.

## ■ Children's writings

Teacher-training courses for non-native speakers never (at least to my knowledge) include information about native children's language learning. Nor are the trainees shown English children's achievements in the form of their writings. The whole emphasis is shifted to the foreign learner, as well as the teacher him/herself, and to what they both should do to succeed. If only, however, foreign teachers were shown samples of native children's work, they would have a better awareness of both the potential and the difficulties of native-speakers, and hopefully, in turn, those of their own pupils. There is no better lesson of what to require and expect of foreign students than to see native children's achievements. The following are the stories written by Primary II, six-year old pupils. They are full of imagination but also spelling mistakes and problems with text organisation.

### Story 1

**Once I met a fairy**

Kate

Once upon a time I met a fairy she was light and bright. she was called Mary. She said would you flate (?). she cast a spell on me. and I began to grow smaller and smaller. and then I stopped. and jumped on her back. she flew up high and when I got to the clouds I saw god. and then I went home and told mummy and daddy. but they didn't believe me so then told me to go to bed I got my pyjamas and then I looked out the window and saw Mary she had to go for messages she was a tooth fairy and my tooth had fallen out. and she couldn't find someone to give 50p to then she saw me and gave me the fifty pence and I said good bye.

(Punctuation has been retained, but spelling has been corrected.)

(the original version)

Once upon a time I met a fariy she was lighet and bright. she was called Mary. She said would you a flate. she cast a spell on me. and I began to grow smaller and smaller. and then I stoped. and jumped on her back. she flooe up highe and when I got to the clouds I so god. and then I went home and told mummy and daddy. but they didnt bleev me so then told me to go to bed I gotmy pyjamas and then I looked out the window and saw Mary she had to go for mesegs she was a tooth faiy and my tooth had fallin out. and she couldint find sumeone to give a fifde pee to then she saw me and gave me the fifde pee and I said good bye.

## Story 2

**A fairy story**
Emma

Once upon a time the Fairy is a good Fairy and the Fairy gives us muney Wen we have our tooth out she or he is very good. very very very good it if they are bad that is all ret (right) but I sil (still?) love them.

## Story 3

**A man and his dog**

Once upon a time where was a man and he had a dog and the man was called Jim and the dog was called Rusty and they lived in a caravan and once Jim and Rusty went out to the shops and when they were out a man went into that caravan and took some money and when they came back they phoned the police and the police said they would come and help to find the money and they came to the caravan and then they went to find the money and when they were going a dog ran out onto the road and they needed to stop and they nearly ran over the dog and then Jim got out of the car and the dog had no owner so they kept the dog and the dog found a bone so they stopped to bury the bone and when the dog was burying the bone the dog found the money and they all went home and had a party and Jim said to the police they could keep the dog and they did.

(Punctuation has been retained, but spelling has been corrected.)


(the original version)

Once upon a time there was a man and he had a dog and the man was called Jim and the dog was called rusty and they lived in a caravan and once Jim and Rusty went out two the shops and when they were out a man went into that caravan and took some mony and when they cam bak they foned the police and the police siad thay wod cam and help to find the mony and they cam to the caravan and then they went to find the mony and when they were going a dog ran out onto the road and they needid to stop and they neely ran over the dog and then Jim got out of the car and the dog had no oner so they cept the dog and the dog fond a bon so they stopt to birry the bon and when the dog wos biring the bon the dog fond the mony and they all went home and had a party and Jim side to the police they cood ceep the dog and they did.

Perhaps these samples should make foreign teachers more aware of learning as a *process* and more understanding of errors such as these, made by their students:

'I wish there wood be pace' (peace); 'I wish I will no die'; 'At first day that was a very hungry caterpilar'; 'chese'; 'stomacake'; 'too' for two. (These examples come from the work of ten-year old Polish children in their third year (150–200 hours) of English.) Or:

'This is the story of a big singer very very good. Michael Jackson song for the once with is one's brother'. (This example comes from a story of a fifteen-year old Italian student attending an EFL summer course in Glasgow.)

The next samples come from the work of twelve-year old children on a Wild West project in a state secondary school situated near the University of Glasgow. The texts are typed and corrected to prevent the handwriting and the spelling from giving any clues. Punctuation has been retained. Three students are represented in two writing tasks: one – a formal letter of complaint, the other – a story which gives the pupils the chance to show their imagination and style.

## Task 1

The bank teller's widow, Mary Anne Sawyer, writes to the newspaper demanding justice for her dead husband. She is now a widow with two young children, Sally and John, aged six and four. She has no pension. What can she do, she asks? She must have justice at least.

Sir,

I have decided to seek justice through you and I hope you will print this letter in your newspaper. My name is Mary Anne Sawyer and I'm a widow. My husband, Patric Sawyer, who was a bank teller, was killed two weeks ago by Ben McGuire, during the bank robbery. The murderer is in prison now, but it doesn't change my situation: I have no money to live on. I can't get a job, because I have to look after my two children, Sally and John, aged six and four. The only thing I could do is to take a part-time job at home.

I hope you will be able to help me and support my request for the pension. I demand that justice be done to Ben McGuire.

Yours faithfully

M.A. Sawyer

(Polish speaker)

Dear Editor

I am writing to you about the death of my husband. He was killed in the bank he works in. He was killed by a bandit who told him to get the money on the till. My husband refused. Then McGuire killed him. So I'm wanting justice for me and for my children. I need money and food to keep us because I have'nt a pension plus I'm now a widow and my children are Sally and John aged six and four. I demand justice.

Yours faithfully

Mary Anne Sawyer

(Native speaker A)

Dear Editor

I am writing on behalf of myself and my two children. My husband was brutually killed in an attempt by Ben McGuire to rob the bank my husband worked in. Ben McGuire was caught but is living a life of luxury in jail. My two children Sally aged six and John aged four are now left without a father and with no money to support them. I demand justice for my family and this is why I wrote to you. I hope this letter will help me to win my case against Ben McGuire, a brutal killer.

Yours faithfully

Mary Ann Sawyer

(Native speaker B)

## Task 2

The public in the town is made very angry at the bandit after reading the letter and form a lynching party. Tell how they surround the jail, oppose the sheriff and deputies and then ...

The sheriff said that only one thing would kill Ben McGuire and that would be the law. Mr Johnston said he had to kill McGuire for ruining Mrs Sawyers life. Mr Johnston ran into the jail and shot McGuire in the shoulder McGuire shouted and the sheriff ran in.
The sheriff got one of his deputies to put Johnston in jail. He opened McGuire's cell door to look at his shoulder. McGuire jumped up took the sheriffs gun and shot Johnston through the heart. He then ran out the back door jumped on a horse and rode into the sun set. The sheriff and his men followed but never, ever found Ben McGuire.

(Native speaker B)

When Ben McGuire was in prison getting protected by the sheriff and his deputies the town were very angry. Thats why they're protecting him in jail. The town got together to form a lynching party. They're after McGuire So they surrounded the jail by having people round the back sides and front. They were everywhere So then Ben McGuire is feeling sorry for himself and he is a bit scared and he regrets doing the crime. He looks through the window in his prison and sees people saying McGuire you are dead. So McGuire was terrified. So then the sheriff said to Ben What are you looking out of the window for Some air Then the two charged through the cell and punched the deputies and the sheriff then got McGuire and said to him you're getting a very painful thumping.

(Native speaker A)

Suddenly everything went quiet. Ben McGuire looked out from the window of the room in which he was kept. From what had happened before, he knew, that the town people wanted to kill him. Now, there was going to be a big fight, and who knows what might happen? He was scared. He was hoping that the judge would not sentence him to death. And now it looked as if there was no other way.

Mr Blake and all the other people began the attack and already one of the deputies was wounded. Suddenly someone shouted:
'Stop the fire! The judge is coming!'
Some people ran away and some stayed and waited for the trial. The trial didn't last long. The decision of the jury spread through the town very quickly:
Ben McGuire was guilty and he was going to die.

(Polish speaker)

The texts were shown to the audience at the CBT Conference. The participants were asked to spot a foreign learner's writing and account for their choice. The formal text rendered hardly any clues, although some participants, primarily native-speakers, noticed different punctuation (too many commas) and wrong use of articles in the Polish speaker's (my daughter's) letter. The narrative piece was more revealing. The main argument – correctness – was used both in favour of, but also against the foreign learner's writing. When some claimed that the pieces that happened to be my daughter's were 'too correct to be written by a foreigner', others argued that 'only foreign learners are so painstakingly correct'. On the whole, all shared her English teacher's opinion that Bogna's writing is very good but lacking in a native-speaker's use of metaphors and feel for the language.

Native speaker A is a girl of Chinese origin, born and educated in Glasgow. Native speaker B is also a girl, one of the best pupils in class. Polish speaker, Bogna, wrote the compositions entirely on her own, during the second month of her stay in Glasgow. Prior to her arrival in Glasgow she had been learning English for nearly seven years. She was in a small group of children I had been teaching twice a week. We had never followed any one particular coursebook but used a variety of materials. In the last year we read together quite a lot.

Bogna's writing, which I consider to be average and representative of children of her age and background, has to be regarded from the viewpoint of Polish teaching at school where emphasis is placed on correctness, grammar and formal style of expression. Colloquial language is definitely not encouraged. School books for her level comprise History of Literature (with samples of prose, poetry and drama from the seventeenth to the twentieth centuries), Grammar with exercises (including sentence parsing and morphology) and a coursebook on style in speech and writing (with elements of narration, description and argumentation).

There is no equivalent to such rigorous teaching of mother-tongue in Scotland. On the other hand, greater stress is put on variety of writing styles and tasks. David Crystal (1987) says: 'We must by all means welcome expressiveness in children's use of spoken or written language and encourage the use of those nonstandard forms that come naturally and powerfully to the child' (p. 70). Will a foreign child ever master these forms, even after a long stay in an English-speaking country? Indeed, is it at all desirable?

With this question we enter the area of bilingualism which is too vast to be dealt with in this paper. However, the fact that children born and educated in Glasgow (see native-speaker A) still encounter major language problems may lead us to consider the question of who is capable of greater improvements – a child with a sound background in grammar, both of mother-tongue and a foreign language, but lacking confidence and the ability to express himself freely, or a child whose power of self expression is natural and uninhibited, but whose formal grammatical training is inadequate.

## ■ Conclusions

Differences between teaching English in the UK to English-speaking children and the foreign learner's context will undeniably exist and non-native teachers have always been made aware of this gap and of their own limitations. It is time, however, to highlight resemblances that would give teachers much needed confidence and encouragement, as it is teachers, whether native or non-native, who bear the ultimate responsibility. Success or failure of certain methods or materials depend on them, their qualifications and attitudes. Therefore, teachers should be helped to explore their potential and not brood over their limitations. The same idea is expressed in The Bullock Report. Seeking ways of improving current standards of reading and the use of English in British schools, it recommended better training of teachers, as 'There was nothing to equal in importance the quality and achievement of the individual teacher.' (p. 182)

Following these recommendations and my observations I may conclude that:

1  More emphasis should be put on training teachers.
2  Teachers should recognise value in different approaches and develop confidence in their own traditions. If EFL teaching, at least done by native teachers in the UK, relies so heavily on mainstream British education, we non-native teachers should perhaps try to refer to our own home school systems and traditions and draw on the forms and content of mother-tongue instruction to utilise them to the full advantage of the learner.

3 Teachers should be more realistic about what young learners can achieve and bear in mind how their students perform in the mother-tongue.

4 More emphasis should be put on spontaneity and free expression rather than just on correctness. Let us encourage our learners to read, speak and write so that they gain confidence and interest in a foreign language before they achieve accuracy.

5 As EFL books have proved to be quite similar to British school materials, teachers should not be afraid to use authentic texts (for example, children's literature).

6 EFL teaching should become more content-based, and focus on general development of young children. The emphasis should be put on work organisation (variety of activities, team work, independence and responsibility of the learner) and on what we teach. Therefore project work, which not only integrates various skills, but also gives sense and meaning to all activities, should be encouraged.

# *Teaching bilingual learners in the UK*

## Rosemary Scott

This paper outlines current approaches to the Teaching of English as a Second Language in UK primary schools. It draws on the writer's experience of working in Language Support at the English Language Teaching Service in Bury. The focus is on both the learner and the teacher and the importance of appropriate materials, positive attitudes and their role in the learning process.

### ■ Background to TESOL in the UK

The Teaching of English as a Second Language in the UK has developed since the early sixties. At that time – and later – there was an influx of immigrants into the UK from Pakistan and the New Commonwealth. This resulted in large numbers of children entering schools who required specific language teaching. This situation led to Section 11 of the 1966 Local Education Act being set up, part of which was a mechanism for funding teachers to teach the 'immigrant children'. These teachers were – and still are – referred to as Section 11 staff, with 75 per cent of their salaries funded by the Home Office and 25 per cent by the local authority.

The thinking on TESOL in the sixties and seventies was that centres be set up where the 'immigrant children' could be taught English for several months before going into mainstream schooling. These centres were often called Immigrant Centres and in some parts of the country children were taken to them by bus. This approach to TESOL, however, came under criticism on political as well as pedagogic grounds. It was felt that the E2L pupils were being segregated from their peers and, in addition, were missing out on regular school work in the target language environment. As a result, there was a move towards integrating the 'immigrant children' into local schools and by the early eighties most Immigrant Centres had closed down. With the development of more positive attitudes towards integration, the E2L learners were referred to as bilingual learners, and teachers were encouraged to look upon them as a valuable resource in class.

Although E1L and E2L pupils were being educated together, there was still a need for language support for the bilingual learners within mainstream education. Language support teachers, therefore, went into schools from Language Support Centres to work with the bilingual pupils. It was custom and practice then for the support teacher to either target the bilingual pupils in class or to withdraw small groups for language work. Withdrawing bilingual pupils from mainstream lessons then became the controversial issue – because it was again discriminatory. Many local authorities were against it. As a result, language support teachers began to target the bilingual pupils in class. The teaching of English thus developed from *isolation* to *integration*.

More recently, however, there have been further developments in the field of TESOL. In order to provide bilingual learners with access to the curriculum, and indeed to develop the language skills of the whole class, support teachers and mainstream teachers are encouraged to plan, teach and evaluate lessons together. This form of team teaching is referred to as *collaborative teaching*.

Fig. 1
## A MODEL FOR COLLABORATIVE TEACHING

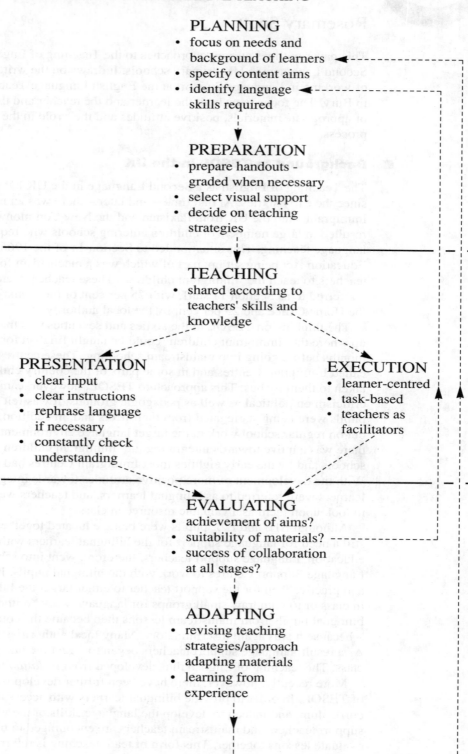

**PLANNING**
- focus on needs and background of learners
- specify content aims
- identify language skills required

**PREPARATION**
- prepare handouts - graded when necessary
- select visual support
- decide on teaching strategies

**TEACHING**
- shared according to teachers' skills and knowledge

**PRESENTATION**
- clear input
- clear instructions
- rephrase language if necessary
- constantly check understanding

**EXECUTION**
- learner-centred
- task-based
- teachers as facilitators

**EVALUATING**
- achievement of aims?
- suitability of materials?
- success of collaboration at all stages?

**ADAPTING**
- revising teaching strategies/approach
- adapting materials
- learning from experience

# ■ Collaborative teaching

The model of collaborative teaching (see Fig. 1) can be divided into three main areas: planning and preparation; teaching – presentation and execution; evaluating and adapting. Perhaps the most crucial stage in collaborative teaching is the *planning*. It is at the planning stage of a lesson that the needs of the bilingual pupils have to be focused on so that they will be able to participate in the lesson. The aims of the lesson must be clear and the topic culturally as well as linguistically appropriate. For example, if the lesson is being planned round a story it is important to choose one that will have general appeal, good visual support and can be easily exploited for the benefit of all the pupils. If, however, the mainstream teacher wants the class to write their own story afterwards, it is here that the support teacher can suggest that they plan alternative activities for the bilingual pupils and other children who perhaps do not want to write a story. If shared planning does not take place, the bilingual children can suffer because their language needs are overlooked.

*Preparation* leads on from planning. Preparation of a lesson includes the following:

- Selecting topics and materials together and discussing how they can be exploited so that all children learn from them.
- Deciding what the aims of the lesson are and what language and skills are required.

In other words, the two teachers have to project what output is expected and the linguistic implications for the bilingual learners. For instance, a mainstream teacher plans a science lesson on 'Smell'. She sets up a situation where children are blindfolded and smell different things to guess what they are. Then she writes up what they have done on the board for the class to copy into their books. This is a typical primary science lesson. What has not been taken into consideration is that bilingual children may not know the names of the things they are smelling and therefore cannot fully participate in the oral interaction. Furthermore, they may not have acquired written skills and yet one of the main aims of that lesson is to read and write/copy from the board. It is one of the roles of the language teacher to sensitise mainstream teachers to the needs of the bilingual children at the preparation stage so that a different approach can be used, particularly for the consolidation phase of the lesson. If this is not prepared in advance the bilingual children will have nothing to do for a major part of the lesson.

An alternative approach to that lesson would be to prepare a selection of smells which are pleasant and unpleasant so that children can respond to smelling them with facial expressions which indicate 'I like it' or 'I don't like it'. In this way the whole class is involved on an equal basis. Then those children who can name the substances do so. In this way, the bilingual children, because they are already involved in the activity, can relate the name they hear to the substance. The input is comprehensible.

The language teacher in the preparation phase thinks ahead to the output stage and with the class teacher prepares a worksheet where the whole class draws and labels the things they have smelt and then the more able children can go on and perhaps do a gap filling consolidation task, preferably from a worksheet but otherwise from the board. In this way, there has been collaborative preparation so that all children have access to the 'experiment' and to recording it. Provision has also been made for a written consolidation phase for those who can cope with it.

As well as preparing the lesson together, teachers must also discuss teaching strategies and their implications. For instance, if group work is part of a lesson it is important to discuss in advance the composition of each group. Very often bilingual pupils are either grouped together or seated in the 'bottom' group, as they are regarded as slow learners because they have not yet developed a good command of English. It is important that groups have a fair mix of ability, culture and sex and that the task given encourages collaborative learning. If the task is not well thought out children may be sitting in groups but working individually, thus being deprived of the opportunity to interact and share experiences.

When deciding on teaching strategies it is equally important to decide on classroom management strategies. If the support teacher does not have equal status in the eyes of the children then problems arise, such as:

- Can she give permission to go to the toilet?
- Can she discipline children where necessary?
- Does she target the bilingual children only during the lesson?
- Who gives instructions?

However, if there is true collaboration and trust, then both teachers share the lesson in every way, thus giving the support teacher classroom credibility.

After careful planning and preparation the *presentation* or *input stage* can be taught in turns so that the message of equal status is reinforced. If the support teacher is providing the input, then the mainstream teacher supports her and vice versa. In many classrooms children sit in groups and often have their backs to the teacher. The language teacher must make sure the bilingual learners are sitting where they can see her, as it is facial expressions, gestures and visual support which aid understanding and help to make the input comprehensible. When children first come to a UK school from overseas there will be a period of time when the language they hear around them is totally incomprehensible, so whenever possible, e.g. during the input stage of a lesson, visual support is crucial in order to illustrate meaning.

The transfer to the *execution* phase of the lesson is made meaningful if the input has been clear. The children now have the opportunity to work in groups or pairs while the teachers monitor. However, this learner independence can only be encouraged through carefully designed materials which are task-based and self-access. Unless children know exactly what work to do and how to do it, valuable learning time is wasted. If bilingual learners are at the very early stages of literacy, then language development activities must reflect this. Examples of suitable activities are:

- Matching objects.
- Fun with numbers.
- Matching words and labelling pictures.
- Drawing maps and identifying countries.
- Drawing pictures/diagrams and writing in L1.

Encouraging bilingual children to use their mother-tongue in school demonstrates to the children that their language is valued and that their L1 skills, e.g. writing, can be of importance in the classroom. Supporting bilingualism in this way gives status to the pupils' first language and raises language awareness in the monolingual pupils.

While the children are working, both teachers have the opportunity to monitor all groups and focus on particular pupils when necessary. Giving time to individual children when a teacher has a big class can be difficult, so in a team-teaching situation teacher/pupil talking time is increased. If it is desirable, the bilingual pupils can be targeted during this period by either teacher while the other works with the other children. In this way the bilingual pupils are having concentrated language development work *in situ*, which is one of the main aims of collaborative teaching.

In the first section of this paper I said that TESOL had developed from teaching bilingual learners in special centres, to the support teacher working with them in class. However, collaborative teaching goes a stage further than that in that it aims to integrate the children fully into the mainstream and allows both teachers to work with all pupils. Thus, with careful planning and preparation, the bilingual children have access to the same curriculum as the L1 children and are not noticeably singled out for special help. In sensitising mainstream teachers to the language requirements of bilingual learners, the support teacher is encouraging her colleagues to take responsibility for them; whereas, in the past, when the support teacher worked in isolation with the bilinguals, many mainstream teachers abdicated their responsibility for integrating and teaching them appropriately.

The final part of the model highlights the need for *evaluating* the lesson. This is where teachers have to trust each other and feel free to comment on the success or failure of their classroom roles. Sometimes a mainstream teacher may feel the support teacher is 'taking over' the lessons. On the other hand, the support teacher may feel she does not have equal status in the class and is treated like a helper. If either teacher feels dissatisfied with the collaboration, it is during this stage that it can best be discussed. Although collaborative teaching has many advantages it is not always easy. Indeed, it may take some time for teachers to feel happy working together and to work out strategies for success. In order for collaboration to be most effective, time allocation for planning and evaluating is essential. A headteacher who is sensitive to the issues of teaching bilingual learners and collaborative teaching will allocate time because, without it, the real value of this approach is lost.

There are, of course, many different teaching situations where language support works in different ways. For instance, I did language support in one class by withdrawing a different group of E1L and E2L pupils every week and doing the same lesson with each group but with appropriate tasks. The whole class covered the same work but in small groups at different times. In this way there was no discrimination or isolation. This form of withdrawal is very popular with children for the following reasons:

- They get constant attention from the teacher.
- They can interact easily.
- The teacher has time to listen to them while they are working.
- A small group situation is non-threatening and children who are reluctant to contribute in class often 'shine' here.

However, if I worked in this way again, I would also like the mainstream teacher to have the opportunity of working with small groups for two reasons:

1  It gives the teachers equal status in the eyes of the pupils.
2  It would give the mainstream teacher the opportunity to see for herself how much language is produced in this more intimate situation. It is also a situation where the teacher can get to know the children much better and, as a result, have higher expectations of them in class.

Whatever the teaching situation, developing the language skills of the bilingual pupils in a positive language learning environment has to be the focus of language support. If this can achieved through collaborative teaching, so much the better.

## ■ Bilingualism

In many countries of the world it is the norm for children to grow up speaking at least two languages. In Britain it is often regarded as a handicap. Indeed, in one school I know of, the record cards of the bilingual infants have 'English as a second language' written in the space for specific problems. In some cases, bilingual learners are told not to speak their own language in school. Generally speaking, there is an ignorance amongst many mainstream teachers of the language and cultural backgrounds of the bilingual learners. Many teachers are not interested in finding out which language the children speak at home and whether or not their parents speak, read and write English. In other words, there can be a 'monolingual complacency' amongst headteachers and staff – both teaching and non-teaching. One way of raising staff awareness of and interest in bilingualism is for the school to have a language policy drawn up by the Language Service and mainstream teachers which reflects the language needs of the bilingual learners in particular, as well as the language needs of E1L children. Although a school with a language policy is one step ahead of a school which does not have one, the language policy is only as effective as how it is interpreted and used. Indeed, many policies are put into cupboards and forgotten about – and so are the language needs of the bilingual pupils. A school with a positive attitude to language development across the curriculum, however, will consider bilingualism as a valuable resource and will do its best to support it or develop it.

The following suggestions are some ways of supporting bilingualism:
• Encouraging the child to read and write in the mother-tongue.
• Having bilingual labelling in the classroom if possible.
• Making sure homework tasks can be done in L1 or L2.
• Motivating the rest of the class to learn even a few words of the child's mother-tongue.
• Keeping a bilingual dictionary in evidence to be used if necessary.
• Sending information home to parents in the language they can read.

In many primary schools there are bilingual teachers who can provide the learning framework for mother-tongue development within the classroom. I was very fortunate to work for a year with an open-minded primary teacher who had two bilingual beginners in her class. These children were eight-year old Greek twins. They had been in school for about six months before I started my language support programme with them. The boys had integrated very well. The other children played with them and helped them. The teacher had brought in travel brochures of Greece, had a map of Greece and had a Greek dictionary which both she and the class used regularly. The twins were always included in groupwork and were, in some ways, the centre of attention.

When I started supporting the boys, I sometimes worked with them within their group if they were doing art or craft but at other times I worked in the library corner with them, focusing on developing their oral language first. I did this through looking at books about Greece where the boys could describe the pictures in English or Greek. Looking at books of familiar places is a non-threatening activity in a second language and encourages bilinguals to speak in L1 or L2. My speaking Greek and having lived in Greece was an advantage. We had a lot of shared knowledge. Like all children, these boys wanted to read and write as well, so I developed an integrated language skills course which first focused on language of description. They were already familiar with the English alphabet and I encouraged them to write in English or Greek. Working with these boys in a stimulating learning environment had other spin offs:

1  Some of the other children learnt some Greek and I encouraged this so that whenever I came into the room I greeted them in Greek and they reciprocated. I also wrote out the Greek alphabet for the class to identify and copy if they wanted to. It was a good language awareness experience for the E1L pupils.

2  There were two Pakistani sisters in the class. I had not been asked to target them, although the younger was struggling with written work. However, when they realised I was interested in Greece they started talking to me about Pakistan and I encouraged them to bring in Pakistani money and any other things they had at home. The result of this was that their identity was highlighted in the class. Up until then it was the Greeks who were the novelty, perhaps because they were beginners but more likely because they were European. By the end of the year I felt that, as well as having focused on developing the language skills of the Greek boys, I had raised the language and cultural awareness of the teacher and the class *vis à vis* Pakistan and the Pakistani pupils.

## ■ TESOL in the UK and TEFL overseas

Whether we are teaching English in a UK primary school or overseas, it is children who are at the heart of the matter. Both learning situations have advantages and disadvantages and both can learn from each other. For bilingual children in UK primary schools there are the following advantages:

• Children are constantly exposed to English, both orally and in written form.
• They are exposed to language across the curriculum, thus acquiring language in context.
• They have motivation to develop language skills, i.e. they need language to have access to the curriculum.
• They learn through experience and play.

Although bilingual children have the above advantages, there are also problems, particularly for beginners. Firstly, for some time this language environment is incomprehensible and this can lead to boredom and frustration. Secondly, bilingual children often experience discrimination from staff and pupils and this can be very upsetting. In the EFL class overseas, on the other hand, the whole class is in the same situation and English is normally taught in manageable chunks, thus trying to make input comprehensible. The disadvantage of the EFL classroom is that there is little opportunity for informal acquisition, and what learners are expected to do with language is often meaningless and uncommunicative. The ideal second language learning environment would, perhaps, be a combination of the two, providing opportunities for acquisition of language in context as well as offering formal language development activities.

# Using video in the primary classroom

Bob Marsden

## ■ Introduction

In this paper I try to answer three questions that you have to ask about video:
- Why should we use it?
- How should we use it?
- What can it be used for?

## ■ Why should we use it?

In answer to the first question, I'd like to take a simple dialogue in its written form, the form it would take in a book:

> *Customer*: I like hamburgers. (*To waiter*) Can I have a hamburger, please?
>
> *Waiter*: Here you are.
>
> *Customer*: Thank you. Can I have a salad, please?
>
> *Waiter*: Here you are.
>
> *Customer*: Thank you. Can I have a drink, please?
>
> *Waiter*: Here you are.
>
> *Customer*: Thank you. Can I have an ice cream, please?

If we compare this with the same dialogue as it appears in video form, I think we see that the latter has distinct advantages over the written form, particularly for the young learner. Video presents language in context and can *show* the meaning of words. It can bring fun and added motivation to language learning.

It can do this because video combines sound and vision. And all the elements of sound and vision can and should be exploited for the young learner. On the visual side, there are people, objects and their characteristics; there is movement, colour, shape. On the soundtrack, we have music and effects, as well as language. In the *cartoon* form, all of these things are particularly strong and clear. The situations and such things as gestures and intonation are naturally exaggerated and are therefore clearer and easier to understand.

In addition, simple language is more acceptable in a cartoon. Finally, the content is more *memorable*, and so what is being taught should be more effectively learnt.

### ■ How should we use it?

As an answer to that question, I will for the moment just suggest three principles:

1 *Show short extracts*. Something between one and five minutes can generate at least one or two lessons.
2 *Show whole of extract first*. It would seem that children do not respond well to stop-start techniques; they like to see what is going to happen, so go back and practise rather than stop and practise.
3 *View actively*. Set a task.

### ■ What can video be used for?

I shall concentrate on six broad areas of language teaching and go through some of the tasks one might use within those areas. As the first use of video, let us take comprehension.

#### *Comprehension*

Video is obviously a strong medium for improving children's ability both to understand language and to understand the elements of a story. Here are a few tasks which should include both aspects:

1 *Gist questions*. Set one or two gist questions before they watch.
2 *Recognising emotions*. Get the children to concentrate on the emotions expressed by what the characters say and the way they say it. Before they watch, ask them to find out, for example, 'Who is angry?', 'Who is happy?', 'Who is sad?'
3 *Sentence re-ordering*. Write sentences such as the following on the blackboard – and make sure the children understand them – before they watch.
   (a)   A policeman asks Bob questions.
   (b)   The King sees Bob and Sylvia.
   (c)   Bob meets Muzzy.
   (d)   The soldiers take Bob to prison.
They watch the scene and have to put the events in the right order. A more interesting way of doing it is to divide the class into groups of four. Hand out the sentences or get each child to write one of the sentences on a piece of paper, so that each group has four children with the four different sentences. After they have watched the scene, they have to change places within their group so that the story is correctly told from left to right.
4 *Prediction*. At its simplest, you explain that you are going to show them a short scene and they must guess what happens next. This may not be suitable for beginners and is best when you are using the video more to revise and activate language.

   For example, the children see the start of a scene – in this case, Corvax sees Bob and Sylvia go off on Bob's motorbike to have a picnic. You then stop the video and ask them what they think will happen. You can make it easier by asking more direct questions, 'What will Corvax and the King do?', 'What will they do to Bob?' Alternatively, you can ask, 'Which of these do you think we will see?'

   a policeman   a doctor   a soldier   a boat   a plane   a helicopter

The same thing could even by played as a game: 'Word Bingo'. Each pupil chooses two words and writes them down. The first one to see his/her two things shouts 'Bingo!' You now show the rest of the scene.

### Language development/revision

1 You might want to revise or develop the ways of expressing likes and dislikes. You write:

Muzzy likes ...                                   He doesn't like ...
He thinks ... are lovely.                     He thinks ... are horrible.

And you might want to give the pupils a list of words, from which they should choose four to go in the gaps:

plums   grapes   clocks   typewriters   peaches   cars   parking meters

You then show the scene – in this case, Muzzy's rejection of all types of fruit and his voracious appetite for anything made of metal. At the end you get the children to write their sentences.

2 You might want to revise colour words. You could give each child a colour and ask them to list all of the things they see which have that colour. You show the scene once, then run through the scene again, stopping to check each object.

3 You might want to develop the description of characteristics, perhaps through comparatives. You put something like this on the board:

|  | Man | Woman |
|---|---|---|
| shorter/taller | | |
| older/younger | | |
| nicer/nastier | | |
| darker/fairer | | |
| fatter/thinner | | |

You go through the adjectives, and explain that the children must compare the man and the woman. You then show the extract. If they have not seen the story before, it is fun to do it as a sound only exercise – you turn the monitor round or put a jacket over it. The children work out which adjective fits the man and which fits the woman.

You now get the class to discuss and you elicit responses – some as guesses. You then show the extract again, this time with vision, and get the children to discuss and revise their previous ideas.

### Presentation

So far we have looked at video as a resource for exploiting language that has probably already been taught. But video is a very effective way of presenting new items of language, for the reasons we saw at the beginning: its combination of sound and vision. Here we see the cartoon form at its strongest. In *Muzzy*, whenever significant new language occurs, the full-colour blocked cartoon of the story is interrupted by language presentation sequences, done in line drawing.

### Using video as a model

1 *Repetition.* Children repeat after a character, either chorally or individually.
2 *Imitation.* Children actually enjoy trying to sound like Corvax or the Queen.
3 *Chanting.* Children chant the lists given on the audio-cassette or in the video. Lists include 'parts of the body', 'days of the week'.
4 *Singing.* Children sing with the characters and imitate their movements. Once fluent, they can do it on their own.
5 *Re-enactment.* Children re-enact a short exchange, using the exact words: for example, the hamburger dialogue we read at the beginning.

### Getting them to talk

In getting children to talk by using video, two techniques can be useful.
1 *Sound only.* We looked at this technique earlier, when used for talking about characters. As well as asking children to describe people, you may ask 'What's happening?' or 'What sort of room are they in?'
2 *Silent viewing.* This is the opposite technique: you show the picture without the sound and ask the children to work out what is happening or who the characters are. Some teachers maintain that this does not work with children as well as it does with adults. Certainly you cannot show such long sequences with children. But it is worth trying, because it is such a useful technique. Apart from its stimulus to conversation, it gives two very important aids to comprehension: (a) certain key visual aspects of a story are clearer when we are not distracted by sound; (b) the comprehension process can be made in two stages – the children can work out the structure of the scene, even the sort of things that the characters will say, before they are bombarded by the foreign language. It is thus a particularly useful way of introducing a difficult scene, whether the difficulty is narrative or linguistic.

### Springboard for activities

Video can provide a model and therefore be a good springboard for a whole range of activities:
1 *Drawing* – the characters, a scene.
2 *Writing* – telling parts of the story; writing a letter to Muzzy about you and your family.
3 *Role-play* – a freer and longer exercise than re-enactment. A sequence is divided into segments; each segment is taught and acted out – but not necessarily word for word.
4 *Models* – make models of the characters; these can be used like puppets for re-enactment and role-play.

### ■ Conclusion

Video clearly has a lot to offer the language teacher and can be used for a wide variety of purposes. It would seem to me that the arguments for using video in teaching children are as strong as those for its use with adults. It is undoubtedly true that some of the techniques which have been worked out for teaching adults with video do not work so well with children, but equally there are ways of using video with children that would not work so well with adults.

## Acknowledgement

Much of this paper is owed to conversations with Barry Tomalin.

## Note

Illustrations in this paper refer mainly to the BBC English video course, *Muzzy in Gondoland*. The video, which is in cartoon form, tells the story of a visit by a lovable alien, Muzzy, to the kingdom of Gondoland. There he becomes involved with the King, the Queen, and the Princess Sylvia, who is loved by both the palace gardener, Bob, and the wicked councillor, Corvax.

# Teaching English through story

Edie Garvie

## Introduction

This paper is about issues and options in the primary classroom where
English is being taught as 'another' language and where story is used as a
vehicle for carrying many important things about language and its learning
and teaching. Story in its widest sense is also the carrier of life's messages
and has, I believe, a vital part to play in the education of the young child,
particularly in the development of language. I suggest that the teacher,
working from a story 'bank' rich in all manner of literary genres and crossing
a variety of cultures, can produce the kind of learning environment which not
only stimulates and carries the children along on the crest of their interest
and enjoyment, but offers meaning potential without which the learning of
language is arid. I hope to show the usefulness of story as a methodology for
the teaching of English.

## The story methodology or 'kit'

To establish a reference point I shall begin by offering *you* a story. It is the
traditional tale, 'The Hatmaker and the Monkeys', which must be familiar to
many of you. I selected it because I have found that young children enjoy it
and *I* like telling it. An additional bonus is that there is a strong story line
with useful places to stop and reflect, places for what I call 'resting' and
'loading', but more of this later. First to the tale.

### The Hatmaker and the Monkeys

Once upon a time in a distant land there lived a hatmaker. There came
a day when he seemed to have quite a number of hats ready to sell so he
loaded his barrow with them and set out for the market. It was an
extremely hot day and the way was long. The man began to feel very
tired. Coming to a shady tree he put down his barrow and sat thankfully
on the ground underneath its spreading branches. He was soon fast
asleep. Unknown to the hatmaker there were up in the tree some
inquisitive monkeys. They were particularly interested in the hats in the
barrow. Making sure that the man was still asleep they came stealthily
down the tree and took the hats out of the barrow. Each put one on and
then they all climbed back to their places in the branches.

After a while the hatmaker awoke. He was almost instantly aware that
something was different. His hats had gone. Where could they be? He
looked in every direction and at last he looked up into the tree. There
were the monkeys sitting smugly with the hats on. The hatmaker was
furious. He scowled and shook his fist. Possibly the monkeys also
scowled if animals can do such a thing. But they certainly shook their

56

fists. Monkeys are great imitators. They copy or ape the actions of others. This gave the hatmaker an idea. He would get them to copy another action. He took off the hat he was wearing and threw it upon the ground. Then he waited hopefully. His ruse worked. The monkeys did the same. So he was able to retrieve his hats. Feeling rested after his sleep in the shade the hatmaker now replaced his hats in the barrow and continued on his journey to market.

What I propose to do now, using this story, is to work through the methodology as I see it, pointing up the possible options of classroom management. At the same time I shall try to highlight the issues of language, learning and teaching which lie behind these options. Consider the following tasks for the teacher first of all:

1 Build up a resource bank of potential stories across a number of genres and a variety of cultures.
2 Build up a repertoire of ideas and a collection of prototype materials to support the narration of stories and as equipment for follow-up work.
3 For any particular purpose, select an appropriate story and devise a narrative which will carry the issues you wish to focus on. If necessary, do the narrative at more than one level.
4 Select judiciously from the follow-up resources for story retelling and possibly for its dissemination into other curriculum areas.
5 Return to the story, presenting work to challenge and extend the original learning.
6 If this particular story works well, consider keeping the materials together in a fairly permanent 'kit', making notes to remind yourself and others of why this or that was opted for.
7 Keep revising your resource collections, bringing them up to date.

Let us now imagine a teacher of a class of seven to eight-year olds at work on the story of 'The Hatmaker and the Monkeys'. She has it in her resource bank (task 1). In her collection also are all kinds of materials (task 2). These take the form of pictures of various kinds, figurines and background sheets for the magnet-board, games, songs, role-plays, etc. There are also a number of prototype ideas for the initial presentation of stories. From these things she will select her manner of narration and her teaching aids, materials for the retelling and those she may require if she decides to make the story pervade the wider curriculum (task 4). It is as though she has selected a vehicle for her teaching which is the story itself and a trailer to the vehicle which is the activity in the other subjects.

Task 3 is perhaps the most crucial, the one concerning purpose. In this instance let us say that the concept of imitation has arisen in a lesson other than English. This had been handled in the community language. Now, in a story where it can be acted out, the same concept is to be dealt with in English. In addition, a unit in the course/syllabus being folowed calls for lessons on colour terms. The teacher sees some possibility here in connection with the hats. She also has an eye on places where position words could be revised, and the function of seeking for information. That is why this story is selected in the first place. But it has to be adapted, to be turned into the kind of narrative suitable for this class. Here now is the modified version:

### The Hatmaker and the Monkeys (adapted)

Once upon a time there was a man who made hats. He was a hatmaker. He had enough hats to sell. One day he put the hats into his barrow and went along the road to the market. It was a long way and the hatmaker was tired and hot. He came to a tree and sat down. Soon he fell asleep. There were monkeys up in the tree. The hatmaker did not know this. The monkeys looked down. They saw the hats. Then they came down and took them. Each monkey put a hat on and each monkey went up the tree again.

Then the man woke up. His barrow was empty. There were no hats in it. 'Where are my hats?' he said. He looked left. He looked right. He looked round about. Then he looked up. He saw the monkeys with his hats on. 'Oh dear!' he said. 'Those naughty monkeys have stolen my hats.' He shook his fist at them. The monkeys shook their fists too. The hatmaker had an idea. He took off his hat and he threw it on the ground. The monkeys took off their hats too and threw them on the ground. They copied the man again. The hatmaker put his hats back in his barrow. Then he went to the market to sell them.

How does the teacher get from the original to this version? Is it simply an arbitrary rewriting or could there be some kind of system? I spoke earlier of stopping places for reflection. I suggest that the teacher first decides what these are by making a précis of the story. She then rewrites, 'resting' at each as she does so to consider further possibilities of learning, and 'loading' the items she wants to use into the new form of the story. Let us see how this works. The stopping-places might be as follows:

a  Man making hats – enough to sell.
b  Put hats in barrow.
c  Sets out to market.
d  Hatmaker tired – hot – rests under tree.
e  Falls asleep.
f  Monkeys in tree look down – very interested in hats.
g  Monkeys come down.
h  Each takes hat and puts it on – goes back up tree.
i  Man wakes up.
j  Sees empty barrow.
k  Looks all round – finally up – sees monkeys with hats.
l  Shakes fist.
m  Monkeys copy.
n  Hatmaker has idea.
o  Throws hat on ground.
p  Monkeys copy.
q  Man retrieves hats.
r  Continues to market.

As she rewrites, our imaginary teacher finds a number of bonuses which had not occurred to her on first sight. Two mathematical concepts, for instance, could be focused upon. The notions of 'enough' and the 'empty set' had been dealt with in the community language. This story could be a useful vehicle for expressing them in English at places 'a' and 'j'. Still with mathematics, but also the English syllabus, sequence words had previously been covered: next, last, etc. These could now be practised again at place 'g'. It can be seen that there are many other possibilities here, but perhaps enough has been said to illustrate the strategy. Just two other comments could perhaps be made. One is that the teacher could use this idea to point up intercultural issues, particularly exciting if she has a multi-ethnic class. In this story, customs of trading and marketing might be explored in an adapted narrative. The other point concerns possible help here for dealing with mixed ability. Different issues of learning could be loaded for different groups and if the differences were very great, separate versions of the story might be written.

To return now to the list of teachers' tasks, let us consider task 4: the story retelling. This relates to what I have called the trailer to the vehicle. An important part of it is the retelling of the story by the children. This is where they make the tale their own, interpreting it in the light of their experience, as Betty Rosen (1988) so ably describes. But the teacher has to make it possible, by her appropriate selection of a story in the beginning, by her careful narrative and exciting narration, and now by offering time and opportunity along with suitable materials for the pupils to make of it what they will. If role-play and/or pictures have been used in the original presentation, perhaps figurines for more flexible manipulation could be used now by the children. For this and the further dissemination of the story, the teacher needs to consider her bank of prototype materials very carefully. If, like her stories, she has categorised *them* well in the first place, then the task of selection is easier. There should be, for example, a clear indication as to which games, puzzles, etc., lend themselves best to an emphasis on fluency and which could be used more for accuracy activities. There should be an indication also of materials which could lead the children on to reading and writing, the teacher bearing in mind all the time the need to develop all four language skills and the importance of careful oracy work before literacy is attempted.

Task 5, the story extension, is an interesting one. By this I am suggesting a return to the original story stimulus after its dissemination, with the object of taking the children forward to more creative work. One way might be to increase the content of the story, using the stopping-places so that the learning grows from within and not just end-on, though the latter could also happen. In our present story, for instance, the word 'barrow' might start off some new work on means of transport. Can the children draw, or tell about in their community language, items of their experience which the English lesson could take up? Can the sleeping hatmaker have a dream bringing in some exciting fantasy items? And if end-on increase of content is wanted, can we go with the hatmaker to the market, and/or, at the other end, explore the workshop and the making of the hats? Perhaps different groups of children could do different parts of this work and the more able not only tell but write, both in groups and individually. The further dissemination of the story carries all kinds of exciting potential.

Another idea is to use what may be called, 'funny visuals/experiences'. In other words, a kind of 'What's wrong?' activity can be carried out. The story which has been enjoyed and become familiar, now takes on some odd features. The monkeys become elephants or the hatmaker pushes his hats in a boat. Children love to spot the difference and especially the incongruity. We should appeal much more in our teaching to the sense of humour. Needless to say, the language needed to match these new experiences greatly enriches the original.

The notion of a story 'kit' is put forward at task 6. But notice the expression, a 'fairly permanent' kit. I am not necessarily advocating a container of equipment, though some might like to have this. (A large see-through bag to hang on the classroom or staffroom wall, with a 'quickfit' set of story materials in it, might be handy occasionally.) But I am thinking more of a collection of suggestions and reference points which could be reclothed, even indigenised if necessary. Take the last point. A teacher in one country does a story about a big red bus. She records her procedure and collects sample materials. A teacher in another country catches on to the idea, but has to make a few changes in the particulars. In her area the buses are not red, not double-decker and not pay-as-you-enter. She has to adapt the original story to make the experience meaningful to *her* pupils, which is not to say that they should never be exposed to the exotic, but that new experience should be gained by means of the familiar.

The final task listed is quite important. The resource banks do change, or at least some of the items in them do. It *is* necessary to keep revising the inventory. The categories in them will change less often than the individual items, but there must be alterations to meet altered circumstances.

### A summing-up

I should like now to try and draw these ideas together in a couple of constructs which I have found helpful. Fig. 1 illustrates the approach behind the methodology. On the vertical axis it demonstrates a development of learning from initial experience through consolidation to wider learning. On the horizontal, it shows the implications for the learner and teacher at each stage. Let me elaborate a little and relate it to my story methodology. By 'field' I mean the area of learning. You can think of it widely, to mean the total curriculum, or a little more narrowly, to mean the English syllabus, or more narrowly still, to mean the overall content of one or a series of lessons, such as a story. By 'focus' I mean the learning issues being carried by the experience and the devices used to make sure they *are* picked up and consolidated. However wide or narrow the field, there is a progression for the learner from the initial experience, where he should not be overfaced with what is new, through time for reflection and practice of new skills, to enrichment of the original learning. Then the cycle begins all over again.

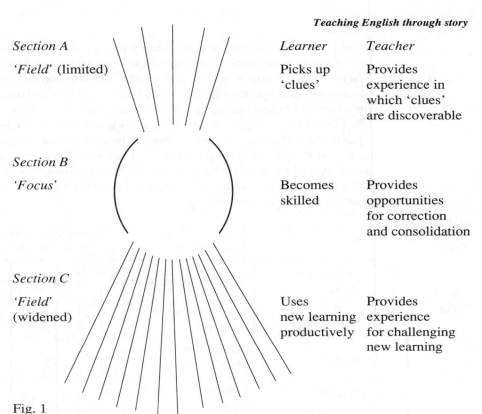

Section A
'Field' (limited)

Learner
Picks up 'clues'

Teacher
Provides experience in which 'clues' are discoverable

Section B
'Focus'

Becomes skilled

Provides opportunities for correction and consolidation

Section C
'Field' (widened)

Uses new learning productively

Provides experience for challenging new learning

Fig. 1
'Field and Focus': A construct for learning and teaching.

It is important to note what learner and teacher do at each stage. Let us consider the field as a story, *our* story. In the initial stage, the teacher narrates the tale of 'The Hatmaker and the Monkeys'. In her narrative she has loaded her learning issues or 'clues' to the learner. In the focusing sessions she selects activities which will make them sure for the learner – the position words we spoke of earlier, for instance. In the extended field she produces her 'funny visuals' and offers new challenge, increased vocabulary like 'elephants' and 'boats' – growing from 'monkeys' and 'barrows'. In other words, this is a construct to emphasise the *development* of learning. It is as though the learner were going on a journey. Hence my use of the word 'vehicle' in connection with story.

Table 1 should be seen against Fig. 1. Here you have the field and focus illustrated once again in terms of the story kit or methodology. It shows the activities and materials opted for, the items selected from the resource banks. Note that those against the focus are aimed at the same level of difficulty and therefore are not in any particular order. At every stage the teacher can opt for one of three degrees of control: directed, guided, free. She can also opt for an emphasis which leans towards fluency or accuracy, and she can select her size of group from whole class through smaller group and pair to individual. The needs of the pupils, issues of language, learning and teaching, particularly those pertaining to the actual situation in a given classroom, call for a variety of class management. There are many possible permutations. In role-play X for example, the teacher guides a group and her emphasis is equally placed on accuracy and fluency. The filling in of the grid for any particular story is a help to the teacher's planning. The completed grid is a useful overall picture of what is or should be happening. The teacher can see at a glance what activities she has covered and how far she is using the possible options of management.

| Field and Focus | Activity | Material/Prop Description | Control | | | Emphasis | | | Size | | |
|---|---|---|---|---|---|---|---|---|---|---|---|
| | | | D | G | F | Fl | Ac | C | Gr | P | I |
| Initial Field | Initial Narration – telling | Set of loose pictures | ✓ | | | Key Stimulus | | ✓ | ✓ | | |
| | Re-telling | Same plus set of figurines | | ✓ | | ✓ | | | ✓ | | |
| Focus | Game X | Photographic Lotto – Moods | | ✓ | | ✓ | | | ✓ | | |
| | Game Y | Snap-picture cards – Body parts | ✓ | | | | ✓ | | | ✓ | |
| | Worksheet | Pre-reading matching | | ✓ | | | ✓ | | | | ✓ |
| | Song X | Zozo the Monkey | ✓ | | | | ✓ | ✓ | | | |
| | Song Y | Resting under the tree | | ✓ | | ✓ | | ✓ | | | |
| | Role-play X | I have an idea | | ✓ | | ✓ | ✓ | | ✓ | | |
| | Role-play Y | See how you feel | | | ✓ | ✓ | | | ✓ | | |
| Widening Field | Story again | What's wrong? | | ✓ | | Creative Use | | | ✓ | | |

**KEY**:

D stands for Directed  Gr stands for Group
G stands for Guided  P stands for Pair
F stands for Free  I stands for Individual
C stands for Class

**Table 1.** *The story methodology 'kit' : Varieties of class management.*

### Some implications of the methodology

First of all, the teacher needs to know about kinds of story and where to go for them. She needs to know how to use the stories that are all around her. She should be an avid listener and reader, understanding the value of the old traditional tales and becoming steeped in fairy-tale and myth, the classics of cultures which carry the universals. She should realise the value to the child of story language, and have in her repertoire the kind of story which repeats an interesting sequence, as do many of the folktales. She has to know how to use the stories of everyday, the ones the children come with, tales of home and community. It would also be useful if she could make stories of the curriculum into narrative at times, not only from subjects like History, but also from the more unlikely ones such as Mathematics. The messages of life are everywhere and the development of communicative skills can only happen by means of them.

Secondly, the teacher must be prepared to give time, energy and skill to the preparation and collection of teaching materials. Fortunate the teacher with an artistic bent, but those who have not should know where to go for help, sometimes using the pupils themselves, who are more likely to become absorbed in a story if they have a vested interest in it. Nor must it be forgotten how important are the teaching aids which lie within the teacher herself, attributes of voice and facial expression and careful use of body language – all the qualities, in fact, of the good actress. For some, these things seem to be a natural gift; for others they can be cultivated to some extent with patience and perseverence and, in areas of the world where materials are at a premium, the story-telling depends on them.

Another implication is the need for a clear sense of purpose. This implies further a full knowledge of where the pupils are and where they are going, so that the story vehicle can really help that journey forward. Because children develop at different rates, the teacher needs a global picture of the syllabus in order to help individuals and prepare groupwork, such as the differing versions of the story referred to above. It is important also to this sense of purpose that the teacher be very much aware of the events of the day and the experience of the total curriculum within the school. Only then can she keep her story bank up to date.

Lastly, the teacher should be conscious of being part of a team. The putting together of a grid, and even perhaps an actual kit of materials, is useful for oneself and also for others. Working with colleagues in the interests of the children is not only beneficial for the school as a whole but is also very satisfying professionally. The colleagues could well include teachers' centre wardens and master-teachers who might be in a position to disseminate the ideas more widely, and librarians who have much to offer, surely, to the use of story in language teaching.

### ■ Conclusion

If I were in charge of the educational purse-strings in an authority, I know where I should be putting as much money as possible. It would be on the support and training of teacher story-tellers. If the teachers reading this article are in the position of negotiating the content of their courses, and if they have been convinced by the idea of a story methodology for English teaching, then I ask them to look again at the implications suggested above and to push for what they feel they need. These are some of the issues which lie behind the classroom options: issues of learning and teaching. There is, of course, a whole other set of issues, that concerned with language itself. The teacher has to be very language-aware and very knowledgeable about the skills of communication. It may be that the tasks of the teacher as outlined here could be useful to teacher trainers as a checklist of ground to be covered. however that may be, I suggest that the story methodology is a must for language teaching. How people think they can develop a child's communicative competence without the messages which story encapsulates, is beyond me to understand. I suppose I am really edging towards the story-based curriculum – but that is a whole new story.

## Note

The versions of the 'Hatmaker' story, and Fig. 1 and Table 1 are taken from: Garvie E., 1990, *Story as Vehicle: Teaching English to Young Children,* Multilingual Matters, Clevedon, Avon. We are grateful to the publishers for permission to use the extracts.

# Beginning a Bilingual Home Support Scheme (BHSS)

## Opal Dunn

### ■ Introduction

In this paper, which discusses work with young learners, and especially young beginners, I shall use the term 'bilingual' rather than L2, as L2 may be associated in the reader's mind with ESL/EFL. These categories, I feel, are irrelevant to the young child's initial learning stages, where learning takes place through experiences in which Geography, History, Science, Social Sciences, Art and Handwork, Music and Physical Education are naturally linked and not divided into curriculum categories. It should also be noted that ESL/EFL categories based on language use within the community may be no longer relevant, as the use of English within some children's communities is changing. This is in part due to the increasing availability of child and adult L1 English TV programmes. In these programmes children are exposed to immersion-type learning experiences, which result in children becoming passive bilinguals. In the paper, the term bilingual is used to describe 'all children whose first language is not English and who are at some stage along the English language learning continuum' (Houlton and Willey, 1983).

### ■ Home Support Schemes in the UK

British education traditionally regarded teaching as a professional activity to be left to the trained practitioner to carry out at school. However, by the 1980s, evidence from research (Hewison and Tizard, 1980; Pugh, 1981) showed that parental attitudes and expectations have a significant effect on children's educational progress. This led to experimentation on methods of involving parents. Most work has been in the field of literacy, concentrating on helping to improve children's reading skills. Results from these literacy Home Support Schemes and Projects have led to further investigation into how parents could be involved in supporting children, for example, in mathematical development.

The main elements of reading Home Support Schemes which have been considered as basic to any Home Support Scheme are as follows.

1  There is regular home–school liaison.
2  There are regular short parent or extended family/child sessions at home.
3  There is regular monitoring by the parent/extended family.
4  The involvement at home is limited to short, targeted objectives.
5  The home tasks are those of consolidation, and do not involve teaching.
6  The relationships between staff/parents and extended family have to be relaxed.
7  The activity has to be enjoyable for the child and parent/extended family, and not regarded as a task that has to be completed.

## ■ Some findings from home Support Projects

Results of research in Home Support Schemes in reading in L1 in the UK during the last decade, such as the Belfield Reading Project (1987), or the Haringey Reading Project (1979), show that where the teacher worked in concert with the home, that is the mother/father and extended family, the child's reading skills improved and the child was better motivated and achieved more. In some cases family attitudes also changed; family relationships became closer and reactions became more positive towards the school and learning.

Kirklees Paired Reading Project (1986) also shows that, even where the immigrant mother did not understand English, paired reading of books in English by mother and child achieved similar results.

More recent experiments with paired maths at Kirklees in the project known as MATHS Project (Multiple Attainments Through Home Support Project, 1986), indicate the same sort of achievement-results and changes in family attitudes, although the content material consists of mathematical activities to be shared, for example, games such as Ludo and Snakes and Ladders, etc.

Research indicates that although the content is important, more important are the facts that the parent gives undivided attention to the child for a longer period of time than the average teacher can generally give to any one child in the classroom, and that the activity provides the child with his/her special opportunities for a physical, caring and loving relationship with a parent or member of the family. This one-to-one caring relationship provides ideal conditions for early learning. It can, in my opinion, be compared to the relationship found in a mother lovingly talking with her baby or between a Montessori teacher and child where the teacher gives her undivided attention to a child whilst he/she uses a piece of didactic apparatus.

However, it is not only the child who gains from the experience. The activity provides parents with opportunities to understand their child better and to develop an acuter sensitivity to their child's interests and daily needs.

As a result of the experience, the child is more motivated, gains more confidence and develops a positive attitude to the content material, for example, story and reference books, maths, etc. The child also increases his/her ability to concentrate, extending his/her concentration span as the project develops.

## ■ The possible relevance of L1 literacy/maths projects to bilingual education.

The results from the L1 projects should be relevant to bilingual education for the following reasons:

1  The child's learning needs and methods of learning are the same.
2  Bilingual learning is related to all-round development.
3  Bilingual education for young children is often holistic, representing a microcosm of the L1 home and classroom learning experiences.
4  Attainments do not depend on the parent knowing the bilanguage.

■ **Why HSSs help young bilingual learners**

Harding and Riley, in *The Bilingual Family* (1986), state that:

> language learning = motivation x opportunity

In reference to child bilingualism I would suggest:

> child bilingual education = emotional security + motivation x opportunity + input.

In child bilingual education the parents and extended family have an important and often underestimated role. The following basic points outline their role.

### Emotional security

The family – grandparents, older children and, more particularly, the parents – are largely responsible for their child's emotional security. A stressed child has difficulty in learning.

Attitudes are formed within the family. Where the family understands the teacher's methods and are themselves involved, they are more reassured and interested, and attitudes are therefore more positive.

Traditional attitudes in society, 'We Japanese are bad at languages', or personal attitudes, 'I was never any good at English', if transmitted to the child, can demotivate.

### Motivation

Motivation is closely meshed with emotional security. Children have to feel secure and happy in order to be fully motivated. Family sensitivity and subtle monitoring of success and failure can keep up enthusiasm and motivation. Insensitivity dulls interest and discourages.

Praise from family members leads to motivation which in turn leads to success: any success recreates the circle. A normal child wants to please and parents' pleasure equals joy and love, which motivate the child and also give confidence. Elliot, in *Child Language* (1981), states that in early communication, praise, resulting in motivation, is more important for further experimentation than the actual new linguistic achievement.

### Input

Input is directed by the teacher at school, with co-operation in consolidation, or support of the child's activities by the family at home. Input can come in many ways:
- *Oral*. Reciting rhymes together, joining in actions, clapping rhythms, etc.
- *Reading*. Listening to the child read stories, rhymes, plays, etc.
- *Cassette*. Listening together. My own research in Japan, where approximately half of the class of seven-year old Japanese girls volunteered to listen to cassettes with mother at home, showed that the half with home support listening progressed so rapidly that, after one month, two natural ability groups formed in the class.

- *TV/video*. Where a parent watches a programme together with a child and later discusses the programme, the results are better. In Niger, Africa, disadvantaged children learned French from educational TV, where programmes were allied to discussion with an adult; without such discussion children could have remained passive (receptive) bilinguals, some achieving low standards.
- *Visuals*: Parents can be encouraged to extend the visual bilingual environment to the home, so making the child more conscious of the bilanguage and the biculture.

Good teachers have for a long time realised the valuable role parents and members of the extended family could play in what has often been termed the Educational Triangle – the family, the school and the child. With the increasing number of young children being exposed to bilingual education, it is timely to think of formalising methods of activating this home support role. The following is a framework for beginning a Bilingual Home Support Scheme (a BHSS) in either a government or private school; it can be adapted to fit national characteristics and local environmental needs.

## ■ A framework for beginning a Bilingual Home Support Scheme

### *Preparation*

1 Begin by explaining the aims and methods of working of the BHSS to the Head Teacher and other members of school staff.
2 Introduce the BHSS to parents/family, explaining:
   - how a child learns a bilanguage. The first stage may be silent, therefore parents should not expect immediate results or show disappointment if their child cannot use English after the first lessons.
   - oral work precedes reading and writing. Oral activities may seem to be only play to children, but in fact they are carefully planned to give language-learning experiences.
   - 'errors' should not be corrected, as the child, as in L1 learning, self-corrects with the reintroduction of correct input. Parents should be reminded of the way in which adults use language differently when talking to a young child learning his/her first language, naturally repeating and recasting language without overtly correcting errors.
   - 'homework' is to be considered as a shared, pleasurable activity in which the role of the parent is to give support. Parents are not expected to teach, but merely support the child.

A typical example of a class lesson, giving details of types of activity, should be given, so that parents can understand the whole lesson programme and not take the child's description, e.g. 'only playing', 'doing no work' to be accurate. Ideally, parents should be invited to observe lessons or participate in a workshop in the form of a child's lesson, and be shown how the lesson links with what the child does at home.

The introduction can be made by
- a friendly letter to all parents.
- a small booklet explaining bilingual education.

- an invitation to parents to attend a class meeting which enables the teacher to get to know the parents and describe the type of bilingual education their children will receive.
- a workshop in which parents participate in activities or in a class lesson.

If methods are not explained, parents may be critical, finding their child is not being taught in the way they were, and feel that 'real' learning is not taking place. Criticism of the school, teacher and methods upsets teacher/child relationships, erodes a child's confidence and demotivates. Once a child senses parental dissatisfaction, it is hard for the teacher to recapture the child's enthusiasm.

### The role of parents in the scheme

Parents often need help in building up confidence that they can effectively support their child in learning a bilanguage. Methods of how to support a child can be explained in detail. Once parents understand that their task is not formal teaching, they are often willing to try. It is advisable that one parent per family acts as liaison with the teacher and is responsible for support activities with the child. However, extra support activities with the extended family can be arranged and are often extremely worthwhile. In my experience, the person taking this responsibilty is usually the mother.

### Types of activity

The following activities can be shared:
- reading together, listening to reading.
- copying activities to make books, invitations, etc.
- illustrating texts.
- collecting items to make collections, e.g. stamps, words beginning with T, etc.
- listening to cassettes, etc.

### Length of time and frequency of activities

The length of time and frequency of activities will depend on the type of activity and age of the child. A parent should be prepared to spend five minutes in the initial stages every weekday, but expect to expand the lenght of time as the child's language skills develop. This would not include the time needed for settling down, or tidying up after an activity. Support is more effective if a definite time is fixed each day when it is understood that the parent is ready to devote complete attention to the child and the child's activity. In order not to be disturbed, the parent might have to make some adjustment to the daily family programme. Parents need to understand that learning only takes place when a child is concentrating. Spans of attention are short and it is best to stop an activity just before a child loses interest. If a child stops when he still enjoys an activity, he will want to repeat it. All activities should be enjoyable and free from anxiety and stress. Where a parent finds a child cannot do what the teacher expects, the parent should not try to explain as her terminology and methods could be different from the school's; instead the parent should liaise with the teacher immediately. Any form of failure needs to be overcome as soon as possible if there is to be no damage to the child's confidence and motivation.

### Methods of communicating support activities to parents

Communication can be by written messages or picture messages. Children can read the message explaining the day's home activity together with the teacher or, if possible, write the note themselves so that they understand the home activity. It is important that children understand the task and are capable of organising the activity themselves.

### General advice

1 For successful learning it is important that parents are happy with their child's progress. Parents are concerned that their child does well and need to be informed of progress. Monthly two-line positive comments in a special letter or book from the teacher can do much to motivate both the child and parents. In some French schools teachers write comments for parents in their child's Agenda; parents reply by writing their own comments.

2 Inform parents of suitable forthcoming events in the bilanguage/biculture likely to motivate them, e.g. exhibitions, TV programmes, new books, etc.

3 Encourage parents to engineer bilingual/bicultural educational experiences for their family at weekends or in the holidays, e.g. visits to travel agents, an airport, a harbour, etc.

4 Encourage parents to make an English corner at home or to collect things for an English corner at school.

## ■ Conclusion

Introducing a BHSS may be difficult and at first may meet with opposition, or comments that a BHSS achieves little and is a waste of time. Parent participation increases gradually. In any group of parents there is usually a range of attitudes towards school activities, varying from negative through neutral to positive. In every family, participation in school activities varies from active to passive. Thus one family might be positive in their attitude, but passive in participation due to both parents working, whilst another might be positive in attitude and also active.

In my experience, change to participation is often stimulated by children. Children are shrewd observers of children and are quick to notice change in class-peers' skills. In a class where a few children progress more rapidly due to home support, motivated non-participating children often put pressure on their parents to begin giving them the same home support.

Where a BHSS has begun, active parents can be asked to explain their participation at Parent-Teacher Association meetings. Parents can often motivate other parents where a teacher has failed to do so.

It is hoped that, by having this basic BHSS framework, teachers will be more confident to make their own BHSS involving the families of the children they teach. Where the child is actively supported by parents with positive attitudes, there is no doubt that the child is more confident and makes faster progress. Where the home is not involved in any form of support activity, the child will rarely achieve his/her full potential.

It is important to realise that the young child will mirror his/her parents' attitudes to the bilanguage and the culture that goes with it. Since it is known that attitudes for life are formed in early childhood, making sure that children develop positive attitudes to a bilanguage and its foreign culture/cultures is important if we are to equip future citizens to cope with developments in Europe after 1992 and in the twenty-first century.

# *Part 3*
# Curriculum and syllabus design

## *Introduction*

In Part 2 we saw illustrations of materials and methodology in different areas of English language practice at primary level. In part 3 we look at the planning that is required once a policy decision to introduce primary level English language into the school curriculum has been made, and in particular the sort of syllabus that might be appropriate. This section also looks forward to part 5, on teacher training and development, in that the implementers of any syllabus are teachers in the classroom. A syllabus designer ignoring this basic fact runs the risk of producing plans that, when turned into materials, are rejected by the teachers. Leburn, as we shall see, highlights the importance of the teacher still further and argues for systems to be set up that explicitly involve the teacher in materials writing to supplement official centralised syllabuses.

What the three articles in this part have in common is their context. All refer to language situations (in Zimbabwe, Zambia, and Brunei respectively) in which there are strong indigenous languages other than English. English is used as an additional language within the country either as a lingua franca or for certain specific functions, and as an international language outside the country concerned. Although the writers in Part 2 of this collection clearly demonstrated the advantages of seeking similarities rather than differences in various Primary ELT contexts, the language situation in these countries does raise some questions which would not need to be asked in English as a second language (ESL) classes in Britain, or English as a foreign language (EFL) classes in, say, Germany. The question whether an 'internal' or 'external' variety of English should be taught in the classroom is just one such issue which is raised by both Hawkes and Constable.

A further common feature in the three situations described is the dual role English plays in the schools, being not only a school subject and a language to be learned but also the medium of communication through which many of the other subjects on the curriculum are taught. Constable justifies the case for English as a separate subject in these circumstances though both she and Hawkes argue for some linking of activities in the English class with the language needs required for the learning of other subjects.

Hawkes advises caution when considering the transfer of approaches to syllabus and materials design from one context to another. He questions whether approaches adopted in situations where teachers may be trained and fluent in the language, where decentralised systems permit a degree of teacher autonomy and where a tradition of pupil-centred education exists can be applied to contexts where such conditions do not exist. Both he and Constable conclude that curricula and syllabuses with an underlying approach to language as communication and interaction (cf Brumfit's article in Part 1) can work in the centralised teacher-centred environments in which the writers operate, but that they must be introduced cautiously and using a model of change which provides for in-service work involving education officers and head teachers as well as teachers.

Leburn, while agreeing with the need for incremental change in line with the culture and the expectations of those using the syllabus, takes a slightly different view of curriculum development, using a 'bottom-up' approach in a predominantly 'top-down' educational system. He suggests that in those situations where teachers have to follow a centralised syllabus and where examinations are based on that syllabus, parallel systems can be set up in which teachers design and produce supplementary materials to complement the official syllabus and materials. Leburn believes that such teacher-initiated approaches increase the motivation and performance of pupils and act as a form of in-service development for teachers. He argues that, particularly at primary level, materials must be exactly right both conceptually and psychologically. Teachers responsible for their own classes can judge these elements most effectively. If it could be proved that such bottom-up approaches influence syllabus developments within centralised Ministries over the long-term, they could be a powerful force for methodology change and materials innovation.

Leburn's experience is based on work with British primary teachers in Brunei who have the benefit of sophisticated support systems set up by the organisation for which they work (the Centre for British Teachers). It would be well worthwhile analysing the conditions under which such teachers work to see whether such an approach could be applied to local teachers in the country concerned, as benefits to the system would be even greater and there would be more likelihood of sustained development over the longer term.

# *Primary syllabus design and materials development in Zambia*

## Peta Constable

I would first of all like to look briefly at the role of English in Zambia and then give some idea of the conditions in the schools and the educational and professional standards of Zambian primary school teachers. Next, after describing the current English programme with its advantages and shortcomings, I would like to answer the argument put forward by Wigzell (1982) that a fixed English syllabus and timetabled English lessons should be done away with in our English-as-a-medium situation. Finally, I will look briefly at the new syllabus and materials which we are in the process of writing. (See Appendix 1.)

### ■ The role of English in Zambia

English is one of eight official languages in Zambia but it is the language of government, administration, law and education. It is also the medium of instruction from Grade One, although one of the seven official Zambian languages is also taught as a subject in every school. It must also be said that the use of these Zambian languages in the schools is on the increase. This must be of general educational benefit and certainly a cause for cultural pride, but inevitably it is also to the detriment of English.

Material conditions in the schools are poor as Zambia's economic crisis worsens: few books, broken or no desks, frequent unavailability of exercise books and pencils, scratched chalk boards, cramped writing and sitting conditions, and few additional teaching aids. There is also the problem of overcrowding in the urban schools, and irregularity of attendance in the rural schools.

Not all is gloom, however. There is an ambitious programme, funded jointly by FINNIDA, SIDA and DGTZ[1], called the Zambia Education Materials Project (ZEMP). This project is reprinting and distributing all the old coursebooks in most subjects, long since unavailable or in scarce supply in the schools, and, at the same time, funding the writing of new course materials to the new syllabus specifications drawn up to meet the demands of the Educational Reform proposals and the proposed move to nine years of Basic Education.

Both syllabus and materials have to take into account two basic tenets of the 1976 Educational Reform Document, which requires that new curricula be production based, the better to equip school leavers for the world of work, and that all those concerned with education, i.e. teachers, inspectors, teacher trainers, administrators and curriculum specialists, be involved in all aspects of the curriculum development process. This is achieved through a system of curriculum committees, which provide a monitoring and ratification role, and writers' workshops, which play a role in the actual process of syllabus design and materials production.

Officially, then, all subjects except the Zambian Languages Programme are meant to be taught in English. In reality, teachers adapt this to their particular situation. Some attempt to teach almost entirely in English, some, especially in the rural areas, use the official Zambian language of the area with a few words of English, while many others use a fairly consistent and intelligent bi-media approach.

The educational system is expected to produce students whose English is both grammatically and lexically accurate and also adequate to meet the communicative and academic demands of the other subjects.

## ■ The educational system and conditions in the schools

Zambia is in a transition stage, moving from a position where there is a dropout rate of around 70 per cent after the Grade Seven exam, which marks the end of the primary cycle, to a system which will provide nine years of universal Basic Education, itself divided into a six-year Primary and three-year Junior Secondary cycle. This will be followed by three years of Senior Secondary schooling for the minority selected after the Grade Nine exam.

The other cause for optimism is that the training received in the Primary Teacher Training Colleges is of a high level and a number of the English tutors have received recent TEFL training in the UK or elsewhere. The linguistic and professional competence of at least the younger generation of primary school teachers is good and their commitment to their work, under difficult conditions, is commendable.

In addition, both at the college and classroom level there exists a climate for innovation so long as it is not too radical and destabilising. Our initial research, before we began to rewrite the Primary English Course, showed that there is an expressed desire to move away from the structurally and pedagogically inflexible approach of the existing English programme with its repetitions and drilling. Many primary classrooms already try to organise some sort of group seating arrangement. Group or pair work is not an unfamiliar concept and many teachers seem ready to accept materials which require, at least on occasion, interactive methodology and include such activities as problem solving, information gap activities, listening to and acting stories, developing personal expression, and giving opinions.

We were therefore able to work from where the teachers were, plus a little more, and to accelerate, rather than impose, innovation in an environment which is reasonably accepting. We are sure that Kennedy's three criteria for successful innovation – the attitudes, aptitudes and awareness of teachers (Kennedy 1987) – obtain in Zambia. We also feel that in our involvement of teachers, inspectors, trainers and curriculum specialists, we are in line both with our own Educational Reform Document and the requirement that innovation works 'bottom-up' as well as 'top-down'.

## ■ The current English as a Subject programme

This programme was written and introduced into the schools in the late sixties and early seventies after the decision to adopt an English medium policy was taken in 1966.

The course served its purpose and was possibly appropriate for its time but it had some major defects:
1 It did not explicitly identify any objectives, either terminal or immediate. The only objectives were the structures and vocabulary listed at the beginning of each unit to be covered in that unit.

2 Language (defined as Spoken Language) and Reading and Writing were seen as discrete and appeared in different Handbooks. There was no attempt to integrate the various skills.

3 The only reading materials for the pupils were a series of Readers, providing narrative or informative text, with a traditional layout, occasionally followed by factual comprehension questions. Everything else the pupils were supposed to do was set out in the Teachers' Handbooks.

4 The course was detailed and also inflexible in its attempt to provide step-by-step guidance for teachers, many of whom were untrained and to whom the use of English as a medium was new. A sample of the old materials in Appendix 2 illustrates this point.

5 The approach was structuralist/audio-lingual and consisted largely of the mechanical drilling of isolated language items, using an approach which did attempt to be situational but which provided little teacher-to-pupil interaction and no pupil-to-pupil interaction of anything approaching a communicative nature.

6 The writing skills were neglected, all writing being of a strictly controlled nature. There was no attempt to develop creative writing or the continuous writing skills required by other subjects. The Grade Seven exam has to be computer marked, so there is no means of testing continuous writing nationally. The result is that pupils enter Grade Eight, unable to meet the demands of writing either of English as a subject, or of the other subjects.

7 The course had neither a cognitive element nor a functional/ communicative one. No attempt was made to teach any metalanguage or provide insights into the structure of English. Similarly no attempt was made to identify the purpose for which any piece of language was being taught nor to use it in anything approaching an authentic situation. The methodology did not encourage the pupils to take responsibility for their own learning, or express themselves independently.

The course did have some good points, however, and the usefulness of these should not be minimised:

1 It attempted to deal with a new situation for which many teachers were ill-equipped at the time and with which they were unfamiliar.

2 It attempted to correlate the teaching of English with the needs of other subjects and to take into account English across the curriculum.

3 It did demand a situational approach to the introduction of new words and structures and in this way did involve the teacher in a more active mode in the classroom than had previously been the case.

4 It did attempt to focus on the speaking skills but relied on repetition and drilling.

5 It claimed to be child-centred and activity based and, while not meeting modern definitions of such terms, it did attempt to provide a wide variety of additional teaching aids at the lower levels to get the children actively involved with the learning process. These jigsaws, templates, flashcards, work cards, sentence building cards and wall charts have long since disappeared, and the teachers find it difficult to teach the course as it was intended. However, the recent establishment of Zonal Resource Centres under the Swedish-funded Self Help Action Plan for Education (SHAPE) should help teachers resolve this situation.

The results of our research into the shortcomings of the old course, our assessment of what the teachers seemed to want and be capable of, and the availability of funding through the ZEMP project, led to the decision to write a new course, rather than to tamper with the old one.

Later in this paper we will look at ways in which the new syllabus and materials attempt to provide a more satisfactory environment for the learning of English in an English-as-medium situation, but first I would like to consider the role of a fixed English syllabus and of timetabled English lessons in this English medium situation.

### ■ In an English medium situation do we need a fixed syllabus for the teaching of English as a subject?

In an article in 1982, Dr Wigzell, then teaching at the University of Zambia, attempts to account for the gap between the level of proficiency that the teaching of English as a subject seems to be able to achieve and that which the use of English as a medium presupposes. He examines a number of alternatives to the structural course I have described and rejects in turn a remedial option, a communicative option, a simplification option, an ESP option or an eclectic combination of any of these. Instead he favours an integration option whereby a fixed syllabus for English would be abandoned altogether, as would the teaching of English as a subject. His argument is that 'if English is to be taught as an aspect of other subjects, then arguably it should not be merely correlated with other subjects in the curriculum but fully integrated with them' (Wigzell, 1982, p. 10). This would involve a radical shift away from a language-teaching methodology which presents language as an inventory of linguistic items to be taught in isolation, towards a methodology which presents language as coherent and meaningful discourse. He argues that all teachers should be language teachers and all lessons should also take into account the linguistic requirements of the topic and the linguistic competence of the pupils. He does allow, however, that problematic language items should be extrapolated and practised in a more traditional way. And one wonders where this should be done if not in the English lesson.

I have no arguments against a methodology which presents language as coherent and meaningful discourse, nor one which makes use of real content to present such features of language. But does this mean we could or should abandon an English syllabus? I think not. Nor, I think, should we abandon the English lesson. And I would like to put forward some arguments in favour of retaining a fixed syllabus:

1 Methods and materials are the *means* by which a syllabus is implemented but are not part of the syllabus itself. The grammatical system of English can provide a useful checklist to syllabus designers and materials writers but does not preclude them from going beyond a mere listing of linguistic items to include topics, tasks, functions and discourse features in the final product. What we are looking for, in Zambia, is a more appropriate and effective methodology along with more appropriate and effective materials. The way the syllabus is drawn up will inevitably reflect this approach, but we still need a syllabus and one which meets the criteria of being finite and classifiable.

2 A syllabus for each subject is required by the Ministry of Education and any attempts to do away with one at this stage would be futile.

3 The English syllabus and the English Language lesson feature on the curriculum of most situations where English is the native language of the learners. Why then do we feel we have to do away with it in an English-as-medium situation? The syllabus in an ESL situation may differ from that in a native-speaker situation, but the aims are surely the same: to improve the communication skills of students both in the written and the spoken mode.

4 At primary level in particular, in an ESL situation, there is surely need for a gradual introduction of language forms alongside the more communicative and authentic exposure to English which the pupils should be getting as they learn other subjects through the medium of English. In addition, in Zambia, the literacy skills are introduced through the medium of English and it is therefore important to relate closely the work of language development with the work of imparting these literacy skills.

5 It must also be remembered that although officially we have an English medium situation, in reality the pupils, especially in the rural areas, are operating in an EFL situation, at least for the early grades of Primary. Some subjects, for example Environmental Sciences, assume that a lot of the teaching in the first two years will take place in the vernacular and actually list as an objective for each topic those key English words that the pupils are expected to learn and use in the course of studying that topic.

6 Neither a fixed English syllabus nor the inclusion of English as a subject on the school timetable preclude a syllabus that takes into account the discoursal features of language or materials and a classroom approach that requires a more interactive/communicative style of teaching English as a subject. Nor does the existence of an English syllabus remove from the teacher of other subjects the responsibility of being at the same time a teacher of English, although, inevitably, the focus of the lesson will be different.

7 It is possible, when determining a syllabus, to work at several levels simultaneously. One can attempt to identify the functions appropriate to each level and allocate appropriate language items to these functions. These language items can then be checked against a structure section of the syllabus. Topics around which these functions and language items can revolve can be selected either prior to or after decisions on functions and language items have been made. (In my experience, the ultimate result is much the same.) At the same time, in our situation, we need to correlate what is happening in the English lesson with what is happening in other subjects. Finally, the syllabus should explicitly try to incorporate the discoursal features of the language. However, it is worth pointing out that the pupils are likely to be exposed to these anyway during the content lessons, and in a way which is genuinely communicative.

There are, therefore, strong pedagogical and logistical justifications for a fixed syllabus in the Zambia context and such a syllabus should meet both the definition of a syllabus given above and the expectations of the consumer. That is, it should be the sort of document that is comprehensible to teachers, inspectors and teacher trainers.

# ■ What is the role of the English lesson in an English-as-medium situation?

If we decide that we need a syllabus in the first place, then it is clear that we need either a slot in the timetable in which to cover the syllabus objectives, or teachers who are carefully trained to integrate the objectives of the English syllabus into their teaching of other subjects. Given that in Zambia there will be no subject specialist teachers before Grade Ten, we do have a situation which would potentially lend itself to a fully topic-based approach (albeit with each subject having a checklist of topics and skills that need covering). However, this would mean drastic retraining of teachers and the redoing of all the recent work of the Curriculum Development Centre, a luxury Zambia cannot at present afford and may not yet be ready for. It would also require a directive from the Ministry.

The English lesson is, therefore, the place for implementing the syllabus. And my contention is that it is the *means* of doing so that is more important than any syllabus-type orthodoxy. Our efforts are therefore focused on the production of materials which promote interaction and communication, and on the encouraging of a classroom methodology which will bring this about.

The English lesson is also the place for ensuring, as far as possible, that English both serves and reinforces the language needs of other subjects. It is precisely the place for extrapolating and practising various language forms; not as decontextualised, uncommunicative, discrete items, but in a broader context of a task-based, problem solving, interactive approach which can be made manifest in the materials themselves and in the type of activity these materials generate.

On the other hand, we are perhaps too apologetic about the need for language learners to acquire a good command of the basic grammar of the language. The English lesson is, surely, the place where some focus some of the time should be on correct usage.

There are, as Wigzell has pointed out, dangers inherent in a communicative approach without any linguistic control. There is the danger that a functional interlanguage will develop through the very communicative situation in which the pupils find themselves in other subjects and, to a certain extent, in the world outside the classroom.

Whether such an interlanguage, leading to a definable Zambian variety, should be encouraged to develop, or will develop anyway, is a subject beyond the scope of this paper. At present, the standards required by the various local and Cambridge examinations are those of Standard English, and as curriculum developers we have the responsibility to ensure that this standard is achieved by our pupils. And it is in the English lesson that we can focus on this aspect of English learning in Zambia, albeit while accepting that as much, if not more, genuine and effective learning takes place outside the English lesson.

The Ministry of Education has indeed acknowledged that much effective learning of English takes place in the other subject areas and, for this reason, the new Basic Education timetable has reduced the amount of time allocated to English as a subject from seven and a quarter to four and a half hours in Grades One to Four.

## ■ The new syllabus and the new course materials

This brings me, finally, to the new syllabus and materials that we are in the process of developing. We have been unashamedly eclectic in our approach. With regard to the syllabus, we took a modified version of the Council of Europe's Threshold functions, treated them cyclically and decided on the linguistic items appropriate to each function at each level.

Almost simultaneously, we drew up lists of appropriate topics and then slotted these into place. Appended to the Terminal Objectives, themselves expressed in functional terms, is a thorough grammatical checklist, for the convenience of the teachers and the guidance of the materials writers. Extracts from the syllabus can be found in Appendix 3.

We have tried to take a topic-based integrated approach, where most of the language work in all the skills centres round the topic heading and where the Listening and Speaking and Reading and Writing skills are mutually supportive and interdependent. We have included activities for the pupils that range from traditional and mechanical grammatical exercises, to puzzles and tasks to be solved, information gap activities, narrative and informative reading passages and, towards the end of the primary cycle, the sort of functional reading and writing tasks they may be called upon to carry out outside the classroom or in the secondary cycle.

From the teachers' point of view, there has been a major departure from the conventional course book. The new course comprises a Teacher's Resource Book and a Teacher's Guide containing the units of teaching followed by sections setting out songs, games, rhymes and stories that can be used at certain points. The Resource Book contains a long methodology section, a short section with some background theory on new developments in learning and teaching a second language, instructions on how to use the new course, checklists of the vocabulary introduced both for Speaking and for Reading, and a list of the language structures available to the pupils at each grade level.

These latter are intended as tools to help the teachers develop their own materials and activities if they so wish, as well as to provide a means of organising revision and tests. It must be remembered that most teachers will have access only to the notes they made at college and to this resource book for reference. There are few books of any sort on sale in Zambia and none at all in the rural areas.

The second teacher's book for each grade contains what has to be taught, set out in thirty units. These units are not then subdivided into lessons, each subdivided into steps. The teachers themselves have to organise this content into a logical and integrated series of lessons, the number of which is flexible, though the material is intended to be covered in about eight to eleven thirty-minute periods. In all cases, the Listening and Speaking section is set out in terms of pupil learning and is expressed first as functions with their appropriate exponents listed after them. In this way, we aim to get the message across to the teachers that there is always a purpose in using any piece of language. We hope that their teaching methodology, supported by the suggestions for teaching activities given in the Teacher's Guide and the tasks and activities in the Pupils' Books, will gradually come to reflect a more communicative, interactive approach. We hope they will move from drilling and repetition to the creation of situations where the pupils are required to be more independent language users, capable of volunteering their own thoughts, ideas and experiences.

In being eclectic we may not please the purists or seem to be up to date with the latest developments. However, from the reactions of the teachers piloting the materials for us, we believe we have selected the right mixture of innovation and stability.

## Note

1  FINNIDA: Finnish International Development Agency
   SIDA: Swedish International Development Agency
   DGTZ: Deutsche Gesellschaft Für Technische Zusammenarbeit

The views expressed in this paper are those of the author and not necessarily those of ODA.

**Appendix 1:** Example of a unit from the Grade 1 Teacher's Guide and the new materials.

SECTION 5: The Unit Plans - The Year's Work.

| UNIT 19: Some things we use | Materials Needed: Pupil's Book. Any of the items under New Vocab. that the teacher can bring in to school. Cards for the Picture Matching Game. |
| --- | --- |

| No. | FUNCTIONAL OBJECTIVES | STRUCTURAL EXPONENTS | NEW VOCABULARY |
| --- | --- | --- | --- |
| 1 | To teach the children to identify some common tools and utensils and to practice asking for something to be identified. | What is this? That/This is a <u>bucket</u>. It is a <u>hammer</u>. Those are <u>nails</u>. This is an <u>axe</u>. | axe, bucket, comb, hammer, hoe(N), nail, paper, saw(N), scissors, slasher, soap, toothbrush/stick, toothpaste. |
| 2 | To revise and extend the children's ability to ask and answer questions requiring a Yes/No answer. (Closed Questions). | Is this your (<u>hammer</u>)? Yes, it is!/ No, it isn't! Do you have (<u>a hammer</u>)? Yes I do!/No, I don't!. | |
| 3 | To give the children more practice in asking about and describing something that is happening. | T. What is he doing? P: He is (chopping wood). T. Yes, he is What is he doing? (chopping wood with an axe.) P: <u>He is (chopping wood with an axe)</u>. | with. |
| 4 | To teach the children to say what we use things for. | He is (<u>cutting grass with a slasher</u>). <u>We cut paper with scissors</u>. <u>We carry water in a bucket</u>. <u>We clean our teeth with a toothbrush</u>. (T.L: What do we use to sweep the floor?) P: <u>We use a broom</u>./<u>A broom</u>. | cut, grass, hair, our, put in, with. |
| 5 | To revise and extend the children's ability to ask about general habits and describe routines. | What do you do every morning? <u>I (clean my teeth with a toothbrush)</u>. <u>We wash our hands with soap and water</u>. | |

# Our duties at school

|  | Dust the desks | Clean the board | Feed the chickens |
|---|---|---|---|
| **Monday** | Sitali | Maria | Chanda |
| **Tuesday** | Zama | Milika | Mutinta |
| **Wednesday** | Chanda | Sitali | Maria |
| **Thursday** | Mutinta | Zama | Sitali |
| **Friday** | Maria | Chanda | Milika |

Read and complete.

1. Who cleans the board on Wednesday?

   _____ does.

2. Zama _____ _____ _____ on Tuesday.

3. _____ feeds the chickens on Thursday.

4. Who dusts the desks on Friday?

   _____ does.

5. Who feeds the chickens on Monday?

   _____ does.

6. Milika cleans the board on _____ .

7. _____ dusts the desks on Thursday.


**Can you read these new words?**

Monday      Tuesday      Wednesday      Thursday

Friday      feed      chickens      clean

83

**Appendix 2:** Present English Course – units from the Language and Reading Handbooks, Grade 4

## NEW WORK TO BE TAUGHT IN THIS UNIT

| Patterns | Vocabulary |
|---|---|
| it'll<br>it won't<br>"-ing" phrases<br>How much .......? | (go) shopping, jacket<br>suit, stockings, shopkeeper<br>shoe shop, book shop<br><br>spend, cost, look for<br>find, cheap, expensive<br>pay for |

### FIRST DAY

### SPEECHWORK

Proceed as in Unit 12, lesson 1, speechwork, using:

| | |
|---|---|
| here | hair |
| ear | air |
| rear | rare |
| fear | fair |
| beer | bear |
| dear | dare |
| cheer | chair |

### REVISION

bad; worse; worst

Refer to the previous Unit for instructions on these items. When doing this revision, make sure that the pupils themselves say the words, and do not merely answer questions containing the words.

### NEW WORK

It'll (be) .............

T:     What's today?

C:     It's (Monday).

T:     Yes, today's (Monday). It'll be (Tuesday) tomorrow. It'll be (Tuesday) tomorrow. Say "It'll be (Tuesday) tomorrow".

C:     It'll be (Tuesday) tomorrow.

T:     What'll it be tomorrow? It'll be ............

C:     (Tuesday).

T:     Say "It'll be (Tuesday) tomorrow".

UNIT 3: READING

## LESSON 1 (45 minutes)

| 1 | Picture Discussion | 5 mins |
|---|---|---|
| 2 | Vocabulary | 10 mins |
| 3 | Reading and Understanding | 30 mins |

Note: Read BASIC METHODS, LESSON 1 before teaching this lesson.

**1.   PICTURE DISCUSSION** for "The Three Goats"

Teach the meaning of the words:

> hill
> monster
> horns
> bridge

using the picture in the story.

**Picture 1**   T:   (pointing to the goats/goat)
What are these?/What's this?
(pointing to the biggest/smallest goat)
Is this the biggest/smallest goat)
How many goats are there?
(pointing to the bridge/river)
What's this?

**Picture 2**   T:   (pointing to the monster/goat/bridge)
What's this?
(pointing to the monster/goat)
Where's he standing?
What's the monster doing?
Are the monster's horns bigger/smaller than the goat's horns?

**Picture 3**   T:   What's the goat doing?
What's the monster doing?
Where's he falling?

**2.   VOCABULARY** (10 minutes)

**Sound words** from "The Three Goats"

> hill
> him.

**Appendix 3:** Extract from the new syllabus

## READING

By the end of Grade 2 PSBAT pupils should be able to:

1.  recognise and name all the letters of the alphabet in English, whether they are presented in their lower or upper case form (small or capital letters) and begin to spell out words by naming the letters.

2.  recognise and read aloud confidently all the sight words taught in Grade 1 and gradually increase their sight vocabulary by approximately 200 words to attain a sight vocabulary of between 350-400 sight words by the end of Grade 2.

3.  apply the phonic rules they learn in Grade 2 (see section on Phonics) to words familiar from Spoken Language work but not previously seen in print and in this way be able to sound out words following very simple phonic rules without prior "look and say" presentation by the teacher.

4.  read aloud sentences and short passages and stories which make use of the sight words they know.

5.  read silently passages which have previously been read aloud as a class exercise, or which contain no unfamiliar words and so can be read silently without such preparation, and demonstrate they have understood the passage by answering comprehensive questions on it.

6.  do a variety of exercises to consolidate their reading skills e.g. sentence to sentence matching, simple word games, exercises which combine reading with following an instruction either physically or by writing something.

7.  answer simple comprehension questions on a passage as follows:
    factual questions
    questions which relate what they have read to their own experience or ask them to give an opinion
    such questions may be asked orally by the teacher or read and answered from their books
    both short answers and answers requiring full sentences should be required as appropriate
    Yes/No questions, questions with "or" and questions beginning with words like: who, what, where, why, how etc.. should be used.

8.  do simple reading transfer exercises e.g. read words given in a chart and expand that information into full sentences, read sentences which contain the information set out in a chart and refer back to chart to provide words missing from the written sentences etc.

9.　　read information set out in a variety of ways e.g.:
in chart form as above
in speech balloons coming out of the mouths of characters in the
Pupils' Books
in simulated handwriting in the Pupils' Book e.g. on the board in the
picture or in a shopping list
the teacher's writing on the board or in their exercise books
in dialogue form intended either as a reading exercise or as a model
for further pupil to pupil oral interaction.

10.　　do the various word recognition tests set out at certain points in the
Pupils' Book to measure their progress at different times of the year.

# Planning for bilingualism

## Nicolas Hawkes

### ■ Introduction: theory and practice

The actual effect of theory on practice in language teaching depends very
much upon the educational context. At one extreme, teachers who are native-
speakers or fluent, trained L2-speakers examine theoretical ideas in
methodology and applied linguistics for ways of improving their own
classroom teaching, and perhaps their language policy, within one school.
Thus, for example, in British TESL for children and in most European
contexts where the L2 is taught by specific choice, the emphasis is on
*teacher autonomy*. Such teachers either follow no set syllabus or make their
own, and published materials are designed to appeal directly to their needs at
a relatively privileged level of resources.

At the other extreme are under-resourced classrooms in Third World
countries where it is policy to teach English throughout mass Primary
education. There central curriculum planning provides national syllabuses
with conforming textbooks, and the emphasis is on *teacher compliance*
within an approved system. Language specialists looking at theory for ways
of increasing effectiveness also work to the system, redesigning syllabuses,
piloting new materials and in-servicing teachers. Paradoxically, increased
teacher autonomy and more pupil-centred learning only come about – if at all
– when centrally laid down policy makes them a priority, and when there is
effective follow-up. The paradox may sow professional doubts in some
minds: why should teachers in African and Asian countries change their
ways just because 'modern methods' or 'communicativeness' are in
theoretical favour elsewhere? Should we speak of 'up-dating' and
'improvement', or of inappropriate transfer of ideas?

This paper draws upon experience in a situation of unusual interest for the
practical study of these issues. Zimbabwe at independence in 1980 inherited
two separate school systems, each partly resembling the cases just outlined.
In the former 'white' schools, now integrated but still privileged, English
remains the sole medium of communication for teaching pupils from a
mixture of language backgrounds. But in the majority of schools English is
L2, Shona and Ndebele being the principal African languages. Enrolment has
increased enormously to meet the demand for universal education after
independence. Though resource allocation is nominally the same for all, the
majority schools have a long way to catch up with the privileged ones. *All*
schools are now part of one national system, including a Curriculum
Development Unit in which the writer was a member of the Primary
language team in the early 1980s. The team's brief was to develop a new
language curriculum for the unified national education system.

## ■ The problem

Our problem was essentially this. The overriding policy imperatives were integration and equal treatment of the two formerly segregated groups of schools, universal access to Primary education, and removal of the highly selective Secondary entry procedure. Indeed, places in Secondary schools were meant to be available on demand. But in this situation of extreme diversity all curriculum planning had to be based on equality and unity, and not on differentiation or appropriateness to different groups. How then could we meet popular expectations of more effective language education across a range of schools varying so much in their quality and linguistic character? And what should the relation be between English and African languages in the curriculum?

Clearly, the main effort had to be directed at mass education, but élite schools could not simply be ignored. Certain features of average and below-average Primary schools, especially in rural areas, were not dissimilar to those observed in the course of experience in other overseas situations: lack of co-ordination between the teaching of the local language and of English L2, and between English as a subject and other subjects taught through its medium, excessive dependence on the textbook, excessive reliance on repetition as a teaching technique and, among planners and language advisers, a difficulty in forming an overall strategy for improvement.

This difficulty often seems to arise when we work with theories deriving from a single definition of what language is. For example, the concept of language as a set of habits expressed through regular linguistic patterns produced a new type of syllabus in the sixties, and for some time actually increased reliance on repetition as a teaching technique. Its mechanical methodology was still exerting an influence, but it ignored pupil motivation, and gave us only a negative view of the relation between L1 and L2. More recently there has been an emphasis on the natural genius of the learner for acquiring language in contact with native-speakers. This definition offers little to situations where there is no contact with native-speakers, but where nevertheless people have been succeeding in learning second languages (Ellis, 1984, pp. 5–7). Of the various branches of socio-linguistics, the systematic study of multilingual societies has been invaluable in providing information for language planning, less useful to education systems at local level.

## ■ Language as communication

However, another branch, the study of 'communicativeness' and language variation, promised by its very nature to be much more adaptable in practice. Provided certain dangers are foreseen, it had already been found (Hawkes, 1981, 1977) to have practical relevance to Primary materials design, capable of useful influence on teachers in a centralised system. It could now also be associated with another positive development in thinking about language: the acceptance of bilingualism as an asset and not as a 'problem' in education (Miller, 1983; Baker, 1988), encouraging different language teams to work in co-ordination.

In other TESL experience, this approach has meant selecting appropriate purposes of communication, or 'functions' of language, expressing each through a suggested form of words or 'realisation', and fashioning the resulting 'target texts' into a consistent plan of development. But this technique can also become stereotyped and too closely wedded to a single concept of what language learning entails, and can ask too much of non-native teachers. It soon became clear that it should be modified and extended in three ways if it was to fit this particular context.

First, in a conventional communicative syllabus, the target texts (based on a description of learners' needs) follow the linguistic and social conventions typical of a native-speaker in the same situation. This is obvious – and not controversial – in, for example, EFL courses for language schools in Britain, but the tendency is found in overseas TESL situations also. We were not questioning the use of Standard English as the target form, but the danger of being too Anglocentric at the social level – the assumption that communication must take place on native-speaker terms. Surely the use of English for education in different cultural contexts requires some negotiation between what is typical of the language at home and what is appropriate to the new social environment (Pride, 1983). 'Appropriateness' of expression in social situations is not an intrinsic feature of the standard language in the same sense that its grammatical forms are (Hawkes, 1981; Strevens, 1981). Especially through examples, we needed to represent *Zimbabwean* communication, within strict adherence to Standard English, the same for all.

Secondly, for Primary children, it seemed unsuitable that our desire for more communicative teaching should be met through the concept of their 'needs'. We were more concerned about effective learning here and now than foreseeing who would need what in the future. Our definition of curriculum covered methodology as well as content. We wanted acts of communication to become a natural part of the process of language development in the classroom. Without this the syllabus might consist of a set of ideal target texts, to be learned by repetition and rote memory, giving the outward form of communication, but having no impact on pupils' motivation or on their active use of the language. This potential weakness has been noted by critics of the 'communicative approach'. (See, for example, Brumfit, 1979; Swan, 1985; Widdowson, 1985.)

Thus, for curriculum planners seeking to influence teaching through a 'syllabus–materials–inservice' model of change, the important message was about classroom activity and communicative learning in practice. The syllabus should be designed to stimulate rethinking of traditional techniques. Functional texts are naturally closer to everyday language than an austere list of structures is, and hence could be a more direct guide to teachers in setting up teaching/learning activities. Thus 'Communicative Language Teaching' becomes a natural ally to 'good Primary practice', and provides discipline and theoretical support for methods otherwise difficult to adapt to schools with large classes and many untrained teachers. Methodology and process were the keys, not syllabus design as such.

Thirdly, a functional syllabus offered a viable approach to the joint planning of the curriculum for English and the African languages. Structural syllabuses had encouraged their separate treatment, since each language had been seen as a self-contained system of forms and culture-specific meanings. The old term 'L1 interference' had been a symptom of this. But the same functions of language may be realised by bilinguals in either of their languages and in ways that are appropriate to their age, cultural context and level of competence. This principle provided a constructive approach to planning for bilingualism, and indeed to the problem of the variety of levels of attainment in English. Children who were native-speakers of English, having remained as citizens of the new country, fluent L2 speakers, and new L2 learners of English could all explore and develop their skills through the same categories of language-in-use. Needs analysis would have indicated different needs for different groups, and hence been divisive. But a unified framework could be achieved by encouraging teachers to be 'functional' in both languages and at appropriate language levels in either. In due course learners themselves adapt their bilingual skills to whatever needs they encounter.

Realistically, the free market in textbooks was another important factor, as there was good local capacity for printing and production. Not only was materials development part of the central curriculum strategy (see below), but clear guidelines to private textbook writers were likely to be well used (see Rubin, 1977).

## ■ The schools

Although the multiracial, former white Primary schools were a small percentage of the total, they had much greater significance in social and political terms, so it is worth saying a little more about them. Most were located in the affluent, low-density suburbs of Harare, Bulawayo and other urban centres. They continued to offer a traditional British-style Primary education to an élite now defined by class and not by race. Many pupils were still minority Zimbabwean native-speakers of English; others were the families of the civil servants and professionals of all races who now took up residence in those suburbs. Such parents continued to assume that their children's schooling would be conducted in English and that learning to read and write primarily meant learning to read and write in English. Civil war and political revolution did not immediately alter that. English therefore had to remain the medium of education, and a sharp L1/L2 divide would have been unreal for that social group. Even the expression 'English as a Second Language' was sometimes in need of explanation and defence, since it could convey the idea of second-class status and hence the perpetuation of disadvantage.

For the trained and confident teachers (still mostly native-speakers) in these multiracial Government schools, the basis for language education remained the Reading Scheme of the L1 tradition, and not the Language Course of the L2 tradition (Kellermann, 1981, Ch. 3). Oral work was organised around the Scheme's demands, taking the Reading Word and not the Structural Pattern as the unit of linguistic selection and planning. A national syllabus consisting of a list of formal language structures would have been an irrelevance here.

Government Primary schools in the high-density suburbs provided relatively good English-L2 (but still English-medium) education for some urban children, while in the country generally there was a great variety of schools run by many different non-Government authorities. Their situation, often in extreme contrast with Government schools, was marked by the shortage of trained teachers. With the introduction of universal Primary education, untrained teachers formed about 55 per cent of the workforce by 1983, and it was they who were most prone to the negative features already referred to. These majority schools were the ones most in need of clear and straightforward curriculum guidance, through the syllabus, the related textbooks and in-service training, to assist their interpretation of communicative objectives (Medgyes, 1986). It would be quite impractical to plan for their needs in a pretence that English in that context could be treated as if it were the mother-tongue. As we have seen, with such diversity in the situation and the attitudes of the teachers, it was a correspondingly complex task to make common curricular provision for all. The fact that English was officially the medium throughout the system meant that policy was simple and uniform, but implementation remained problematic.

## ■ The new language curriculum

What then was the policy position with regard to the African languages? In the majority schools, the soundest and most practical step would surely have been a reassertion of Shona and Ndebele as part of the new dignity of African culture, no longer subservient to white rule. But in fact this could be done only on a modest scale, for reasons similar to those just referred to. The impetus towards equality of access for all races meant that English was still seen as the key to opportunity. Hence there could not be two official categories of school, one English-medium, the other African-language-medium, any more than there could be 'L1' versus 'L2' treatment of English. Moreover, the socialist principles on which the Government had come to power favoured modernism over indigenous tradition in matters where the two might be in conflict. Government therefore did not lay heavy emphasis on languages associated with cultural traditions, some of which it regarded as backward-looking and out of keeping with the new political values. Nevertheless African language syllabuses and materials were developed by the Curriculum Unit (mentioned briefly below).

But first let us look at the curriculum which was eventually developed, after much drafting and trialling, for English language. Though it was designed to suit specific educational and cultural needs, the principles employed are adaptable to language education in other non-Western contexts. As important as the syllabus itself were the methods adopted for development and dissemination, described below.

Appendix 1 shows typical units from the syllabus. It was deliberately divided into a series of discrete units, each unit (read from left to right) having a *functional* element, expressed as an objective, a *structural* element, and notes on *methodology*. Thus the communicative function is the basis of the unit, and from it are derived the language items in the centre column. These are regarded as a minimum expression of the objective, probably appropriate to teachers of most L2-majority children. Where grammatical structures occur for the first time, they are then explicitly listed for reinforcement at the end of each half-termly block of units, and in summary at the end of the year.

Other features of the design were *linguistic flexibility, sequencing*, and *cultural content*. The *flexibility* of a function-based syllabus has already been noted. Now in detail we see that functions such as 'give simple directions' or 'identify oneself as a member of a group', can be expressed in simple or more complex ways; children with greater access to English can learn to communicate in freer language than the minimum indicated in Units 4.c

(Grade 3) and 2.b (Grade 4) respectively. Those with great fluency or near-native command can be given guidance in developing their accuracy or expressiveness in realising the same communicative objectives. But the relatively detailed specification of language items means that diffident or untrained teachers do receive help and support, which they would not receive from looser guidelines requiring more interpretation.

It may be objected that no guidance is in fact offered beyond the minimum, but we had observed that it is easier for the language level to 'float upwards' naturally in favourable situations than to be restricted by the teacher in unfavourable ones. We therefore planned for the latter in the Core Units, judged by our classroom trials to require half to two-thirds of the available teaching time. A separate 'Enrichment' section catered directly for teachers in more English-oriented schools, listing further optional functions and activities appropriate to their needs, to be taken up in the remaining time. The ongoing Core Units assume only a mastery of previous Core material.

As for *sequence*, it has been observed (Johnson, 1981, pp. 92–94) that functional units do not naturally fall into any particular sequence. But here the grammatical structures derived from the functions were used in a quite traditional way as the basis for grouping and sequencing the units within the year. Simple structures preceded more complex ones, and new items were spread as evenly as possible. Needless to say, structures once introduced recur constantly, so the effect is spiral not linear, and revision is inbuilt. But we did not impose a rigid sequence even so; teachers select their own order of units within each half-termly block (six per year).

On the *cultural aspect*, the language is located in situations which are indentifiably Zimbabwean in character, socially and in the references they make, thus avoiding the sort of Anglocentrism discussed earlier. Emphasis is placed on rural life, on an implicit equality of value and esteem for all groups in society, and on co-operation for common ends: all in contrast to the values of the colonial society, and consistent with the character of all the new syllabuses and materials at that time. The method notes and the fact that the syllabus is conventionally organised in discrete units were essential to the process of disseminating it and its methodology through in-service workshops, and to liaison with pre-service training in the Colleges. Subsequent commercial textbooks have exploited these principles appropriately.

One aspect of language development represented only in the English syllabus was that of its use as the *medium of instruction*. Since English has that role officially in all schools, some account had to be taken of language across the curriculum. We were especially concerned to anticipate L2 pupils' encounters with new concepts and new learning processes in other subjects through their weaker language, although we could not meet the integrated cross-curricular ideal advocated by Dallas and Williams (in Alderson and Urquhart, 1984). This servicing of the medium of instruction became stronger from Grade 4 onwards, as the cognitive load carried by English increased. Examples of this for Social Studies and Agriculture can be seen in Units 2.a and 5.b of Grade 4 (Appendix 1). While effectiveness inevitably depends on the teachers, our overall strategy was to make provision in the earlier years for the language of personal interaction and self-expression, and later for extending them, and for more academic uses of language. (Cummins, 1984). Simultaneously with this development comes increased reliance on reading and writing in acquiring and expressing knowledge, at the expense of listening and speaking.

However, it is the content-subject lessons themselves which are the main opportunity to work for this extension of language and cognitive skills. It is essential that the teacher sees those lessons as part of the process of strengthening linguistic ability, not for content-teaching alone, and not assuming that the necessary linguistic knowledge and skills are already in place. This is a factor in education in any language, and an even greater one in a bilingual context, as Cummins (op. cit.) has rightly warned. There is a need for co-ordination between teachers from one grade to the next, as well as between the teaching of two languages taught by the same teacher to the same class.

As for the African languages, work on the Shona and Ndebele syllabuses, in which the writer was not directly involved, proceeded in parallel with English. These likewise listed functional modes of language use, showing how children may develop their mother-tongue on the basis of a systematic description of communicative functions. Language development is again seen in relation to the socio-cultural context, broken down into domains, which are recycled through the Primary grades as a sort of spiral curriculum. Care was taken that the African languages and English should not be polarised into representing a traditional rural way of life and a modern urban one respectively. Hence exemplification of English covers many local settings, including some in which English would not normally be used, and Shona and Ndebele are sometimes seen in use in offices, for example, or on the telephone or in discussion of current topics, a mixture of new and old appropriate to a changing society. Finally, since there are major dialect areas within Shona and within the Zulu group which includes Ndebele, teaching children competence in the standard dialect is an important element in schooling. This requires a separate section on grammatical accuracy in each African language syllabus. Hence both function and form are covered in L1 and in L2.

## ■ Style of innovation

In any curriculum development, it is important that the style adopted in the dissemination of change should be in harmony with the nature of the particular innovation itself. This principle may seem obvious, but is not always observed in practice. Over twenty years ago the writer had seen 'New Maths' innovators promoting 'activity methods' and 'the importance of concept formation' by exhortation from the platform, rather than by practising in the field what was being preached for the classroom. Yet avoiding this trap is not easy for even the most conscientious curriculum developers carrying authority in a centralised system. The dilemma is all the more acute when teachers themselves by habit adopt the attitude of 'You tell us, and we'll try to comply'. Rather than seeking compliance with an imposed programme, the specialist team needs to involve a wide spectrum of teachers, Heads and Education Officers in working out the implications of what they are proposing, within the inevitable budgetary limits.

In our case, the commitment to the principles of communication and active involvement at all levels was expressed in two ways: a two-year series of regional workshops for Primary Heads, representative class teachers and

Education Officers, and classroom trials of new Teaching Units, written by ourselves to exemplify the syllabus units and thus increase understanding of the changes we were trying to bring about.

Rather than plan the curriculum entirely from the centre, we drew up draft lists of the functional objectives, and of contexts for their application and use. These lists we took with us on workshops round the country, approximately one grade per region. Participants worked in groups to select the objectives which they judged suitable to the age/grade level, in terms of content, language and culture. We also tried out the actual form of presentation used in the syllabus document, eventually as shown in Appendix 1. At the same workshops and at other in-service courses, we demonstrated and practised with teachers the methodology and lesson-planning needed to implement the units. Most of them require five to six lesson periods to teach. It was particularly important that the teacher should not plunge straight into the target activity, but should build up towards it.

The sample Teaching Units were complete with pupil materials, and represented a venture into public-sector writing in parallel with what the commercial publishers would do later. The training of writers under the aegis of the Ministry of Education was one of the basic aims of the project, as well as the actual production of materials. The scale of the operation was small, but nevertheless useful in showing how pupils and teachers responded to the new communicative activities and to the formal element. Their responses were consistently positive; and observing and discussing lessons with pilot teachers was invaluable for the curriculum writers. The experience also provided feedback on how much the average class could be expected to cover in a given time, an important check against overload. (It is extraordinary how rare this type of syllabus evaluation is.) All that has happened since suggests that that our socio-linguistic and methodological approach had an appropriate theoretical orientation, providing a versatile and sensitive framework within which to tackle the challenges presented in multicultural Zimbabwe after independence.

**Appendix 1:** Units from the Zimbabwe Primary English Course

| FUNCTIONAL OBJECTIVE | STRUCTURE AND VOCABULARY | LANGUAGE TASK |
|---|---|---|

Primary Three

### Unit 4. c

| | | |
|---|---|---|
| Give simple directions on how to find a familiar place. | **X:** How do I get to (the market) place?<br>*or* Which way is it to (the Chief's house), please?<br><br>**Y:** Go down/up this road to (the store).<br>At the (store), turn left/right and walk about (500) metres. You will see (the market) on your (right).<br><br>(Enquirer then repeats instructions as a check).<br><br>**X:** Thank you very much.<br><br>*Also* Go straight down/up the road......................<br>**N.B.** The above are a simple form of directions, using imperative. You will have to adapt them to your locality. | Start by giving directions within the school itself.<br><br>Then use a blackboard map of the area as an aid: one pupil gives the directions, another follows, using a chalk line on the map.<br><br>Then go out of the school, and practise full dialogue, with greetings, etc, as if speaking to a stranger. |

### Unit 5. c

| | | |
|---|---|---|
| **A.** Give names of various machines, especially those involved in Education and with Production and with rural development. | This is a rake/trowel/hand-fork/watering-can/saw.<br><br>These are our tools.<br>We have a (rake).<br>We have some string/fertiliser/manure.<br><br>That's a (tractor) over there. | Describe pictures of farm equipment, and take a "language walk" to look at tools. (These should be tools belonging to your school for Education with Production. If not, locate others.) |
| **B.** Ask and answer about tools and machines and what they are used for. | What is a (watering-can/saw/tractor) used for?<br>It's used for (watering/cutting wood/pulling the plough).<br><br>Is it broken?  Yes it is.<br>We must mend it/get another one.<br>*or*  No it isn't all right.<br><br>How do you look after it?...................... | Pair-work by pupils, asking and answering about tools, or pictures of tools and machines.<br><br><br>**Common tools:** axe, hammer, fork, saw, bucket, cart, badza, spade, wagon, watering-can, lorry, wheelbarrow, tractor, truck, trowel, plough. |

| FUNCTIONAL OBJECTIVE | STRUCTURE AND VOCABULARY | LANGUAGE TASK |
|---|---|---|

**Primary Four**

### Unit 2. a

| | | |
|---|---|---|
| State the conditions under which a change will take place, and the results of possible courses of action. | If you (space out the seedlings), they will (grow better).<br><br>If we don't (take care, the disease) will (spread).<br><br>E.g.<br>If we sell the crop, the school will have money for ..................................<br><br>But if we eat it, we shall enjoy the good food!<br><br>If the tomatoes ripen in the holidays, who will pick them? | Relate to observation of the environment, especially where children are doing practical work, or engaged in a project.<br><br>Groups consider what the best course of action will be, by balancing the alternatives.<br><br>Short written account of and problem faced by your group. |

### Unit 2. b

| | | |
|---|---|---|
| Identify themselves as members of various groupings: family, age-group, class, school, village, neighbourhood, town, nation. | My father/mother is .............................<br>My elder brother is ...........................(etc).<br>I am the eldest/youngest(third) in my family.<br><br>My friends are ............... and .....................<br>We meet at ............. 's house.<br>We usually ..... together.<br><br>This is grade 4.c.<br>Our teacher is Cde (Murisa).<br>Our classroom is ..................................<br><br>We go to .....School, in (Midlands) Province.<br>The Headmaster/Headmistress is Cde (J.R. Cumbo).<br>The school has (820) pupils.<br><br>Our family belongs to the Co-operative.<br>(etc. about other groupings). | Relate to social studies. Develop the consciousness of individual pupils as members of groups to which they have responsibility. See individual progress or achievement in terms of group progress or achievement, not for oneself alone. Get true instances from pupils of groups, clubs and other organisations. |

### Unit 5. b

| | | |
|---|---|---|
| Identify places used by the community as a whole, or by groups within the community neighbourhood. | We/I live in....................It is a part of...................../or a village in .................... area.<br><br>All the families know each other in ...................<br>People greet one another/each other in the mornings.<br><br>We have a market/well/borehole/dam/ community centre/culture house/playground/ church/library/cooperative/police station.<br><br>The community wants to improve itself.<br>We want to improve ourselves. | Relate the Unit specifically to the community which your school serves and to aspects of the Social studies syllabus. Devise such activities as making a plan of the area, with the buildings marked; talking to people who work at each place (see Unit 5f); children saying when they have been to them before; making written reports. |

# Materials writing: setting the wheels in motion

## Hugh Leburn

### ■ Introduction

A writer concluded in a recent article: 'No materials can ever be truly "communicative" when they are mass-produced for mass sales in many different countries of the world.' This statement confirmed one of the principles behind the materials writing on the Centre for British Teachers Primary project in Brunei Darussalam, and contributes to the main contention of this paper, namely that materials writing, by teachers, is often the best way of setting the wheels of improvement in motion. I shall be writing with particular reference to Brunei, but the principles can be applied to other situations. I shall argue, too, that some of the benefits are not directly related to materials. The teachers on the project in Brunei are British, working in state schools in Brunei. Even greater benefits might accrue if the principles were applied on a project for local teachers.

### ■ Bruneian requirements

Brunei Darussalam is a small country of fewer than a quarter of a million people. It achieved independence in the early 1980s after having the status of a British Protectorate for most of the century.

I would like to present a number of items from the national syllabuses and the national exams:

| 83 | 'Will be'  Future Tense | It will be Friday tomorrow. |
| | | Tomorrow will be Muharram. |
| | | The month after Ramadhan will be Shawal. |
| | | It will be the end of term holiday next month. |
| 84 | The Present Simple Tense (universals) | The earth goes round the sun. |
| | | All insects have three pairs of legs. |
| | | Animals and plants need oxygen to live. |

This is an extract from the grammar part of the Primary 4 English syllabus. The pupils will be nine to ten years old, unless they have repeated any of the previous three years. Two and a half hours a week is normally allotted to grammar and, with tests and exams to be fitted in, a unit corresponds roughly to a week. The syllabus is somewhat fragmented.

| | |
|---|---|
| Syllabus content: | Why teach History? |
| Rationale: | Pupils should be taught what history is about, and why we study history. The understanding of pupils in the aforementioned points would serve as a guide towards the learning of the topics that follow. |
| Aims: | This title aims to provide an understanding of the following: |

1.1 History relates to true occurrences or events pertaining to mankind.

1.2 Every historical event has its beginning and origin, the development of which is continuous and this encompasses three chronological stages, i.e. the past, the present and the future.

1.3 History gives us knowledge, encouragement, guidance and thoughts of mankind to improve our way of life.

This extract is from the Teacher's Guide for the Primary 4 History syllabus. Originally designed for Primary 5 pupils who had achieved good enough marks to study Maths, Science, Geography and History in English, it is now used, since the introduction in 1985 of a bilingual policy for all pupils, in Primary 4. There is no textbook and teachers are often reduced to presenting the content of the Teacher's Guide as material for the pupils, who understand neither the language, the content nor the concept. The final sentence has appeared in exams, with True/False written after it. With some pupils remembering having seen the sentence in their copied notes, the success rate on this question can be high. A new History syllabus is in preparation.

Write a composition of about 150 words on one of the following:

1 My House

2 My Little Brother

3 My Little Sister

4 My pet

5 My Hobby

This is the English Composition Paper of the National Exam taken at the end of the Primary school, in Primary 6 or Primary 7. The titles change little from year to year and are predicted by teachers who give model answers to their pupils to be learnt by heart.

i    How many girls are there in your class?

     _____ ten girls.

a)   There is

b)   There are

c)   There was

d)   There were

ii   _____ the name of this animal?

a)   Does you know

b)   Does they know

c)   Did you know

d)   Do you know

This is from the same National Exam, the Primary Certificate of English exam. Grammar is a major part of the exam. Syntax is specifically tested in another section.

Camels are animals found in the continents of Asia and Africa. The camel is well-known for its usefulness for carrying heavy loads across dry places, especially deserts, and is often called the ship of the desert. It is an animal with very wide feet which enable it to walk easily on sand. It can also travel for long distances without drinking water.

1   In which continents are camels found?

2   What is the camel well-known for?

3   What is the camel often referred to? (*sic*)

The Comprehension passage requires, again in the same exam, full sentences to be written. Scanning and copying out the relevant sentence will often bring marks, but where more sophisticated skills are needed and possibly used, the need to compose correct answers is often the stumbling block.

## ■ The wrong conclusions

It is very easy to draw the wrong conclusion from what has been shown above. It would be easy to react by suggesting that a more communicative syllabus should be written immediately, or that a more modern approach to exams should be implemented forthwith, or that more money should be spent on resources, or even that someone from outside should advise on the necessary changes.

Yet none of these suggestions would be helpful or relevant, for they fail to consider the Bruneian situation and view. In a country which has seen the school population quadruple in thirty years, it has been a major achievement to build sufficient schools and train enough teachers, and familiar syllabuses and exams provide a stable band of expectations and objectives.

Nor are outpourings of money likely to be the answer. Such textbooks, videos, tapes, readers, posters as could be purchased are unlikely, with the exception of certain readers, to cover all the requirements of fitting the syllabus: being appropriate for Muslim learners, being accessible to pupils on this South East Asian island, in terms of content and language level, and being operable by local teachers.

Bruneians wish to carry out their education policy their way, and such changes as may be required can only come from within their system and on their initiative.

## A possible solution – CFBT's role

The Centre for British Teachers Primary project was set in motion by the Ministry of Education in response to a shortage of English teachers in Primary schools, caused by the introduction of bilingual education for all pupils at Primary 4, and by a concern for the standard of English in the schools, which was to be overcome by trained native-speakers. Although the original purpose for the project has not changed, there is now some desire for the professional practice and techniques of these teachers.

All 120 CFBT Primary teachers teach English to upper Primary classes. In the first two years of the project, when the numbers were fewer, they taught all five English-medium subjects. The majority of the teachers have Primary training and experience as well as an RSA (Prep) Certificate, which they do before coming to Brunei. Others have some experience of EFL, but perhaps little or no experience of young learners. An important feature of teachers' work has been the synthesis of Primary practice and EFL methodology, and of European ideas and Bruneian targets.

The position of the CFBT teachers is an interesting one. They work in the system and yet they are not part of the system, not being under direct contract to the government and being expatriate. On the one hand, this has allowed them to have first hand experience of the situation, while being part of an independent body; on the other hand, being expatriate will always reduce the validity of what they do.

Such a large body of teachers provides an opportunity to function productively. Materials writing was chosen as the central vehicle for the productivity of the project for a number of reasons. First, it was where the greatest need was; second, it was directly relevant to the reaction of the pupils and their needs; third, it was seen as a way of helping training and teacher development; fourth, it was in line with past CFBT experience that, while tapping the combined potential of the group, it also fostered the co-operative instinct; and fifth, it could show those with whom and for whom the teachers were working what they were doing and what they were capable of.

## Factors affecting materials production

I have listed below the factors that guided the materials production carried out on the project in Brunei. They are a response to the situation there. Among the motivating factors the need for materials was first and foremost a priority because there was no purpose-written textbook, and the following factors reflected the fact that such materials as did exist were not suitable for the pupils from a number of angles.

The constraining factors might be common to the situation of many countries all over the world and might well act as a basic guide. The combination of motivating and constraining factors is a practical one. It ensures a positive and usable response and resource in any situation.

### Motivating factors

1  The need for materials.
2  The need for materials at the language level of Bruneian Primary pupils.
3  The need for materials at the right conceptual level for Primary pupils.
4  The need for materials at the right psychological level for Primary pupils:
    (a) activity-based
    (b) visually supportive
    (c) providing variety
    (d) ensuring success
    (e) containing an element of task/quiz/competition.
5  The need for materials that develop:
    (a) deductive and inductive powers
    (b) imagination
    (c) oral fluency
    (d) the concept of English as something to be used.

### Constraining factors

1  The need to follow the syllabus.
2  The need to prepare pupils for national exams.
3  The availability of resources.
4  The expectations of local colleagues.
5  The conditions of schools.
6  The procedures in schools.
7  The need to introduce innovations slowly and sensitively.
8  The need to work in line with the accepted precepts and culture of the country.

## ■ Samples of materials

Below is a list of sample materials (reproduced in Appendix 1), together with the name of the writer and some comments that illustrate how the motivating and constraining factors combined to produce the material. All materials have been distributed to schools through various CFBT publications.

1  *Cue Sheet for Primary 6, Item 135* by Janice Collins
    Follows the syllabus; visually supported; easy enough to ensure success; graded to be usable with mixed ability classes; develops deductive operation.
2  *Sources of Light* by Dee Dunstan
    Follows Science syllabus item; visually supported; develops inductive powers; English as a medium.
3  *Panglima Beruddin* by Jenny Wade
    Follows History syllabus item; visually supported; activity based; element of task; possibly encouraging imagination.
4  *Agricultural Products of Malaysia* by Hugh Leburn
    Follows Geography syllabus item; visually supported; simplified language structure; element of task.

5  *Family Tree* by Jan Wells
   Right language level; right conceptual level; element of task; deductive powers being used.
6  *Mime to Practise Phrasal Verbs* by Eunice Stephen
   Follows syllabus item; helps oral fluency; activity based; encourages development of imagination; visually supported.
7  *The Old Man* by David Blackwell
   Right language level; suitable for mixed ability; ensures success.
8  *The Grandfather* by Anne Graham
   Helps preparation for National Exam; visual stimulus; accessible to pupils' experience; helps oral fluency; could develop imagination.

## ■ Organisation of materials writing

Materials writing can be diverse. Any programme of materials writing has to contain a framework that allows decisions to be made on what should be designed and how it should be produced. The starting points for materials writing are, first, where there are gaps and, second, where some kind of discussion or input suggests the possibility of trying out something new. This is illustrated in Fig. 1.

**Fig. 1**

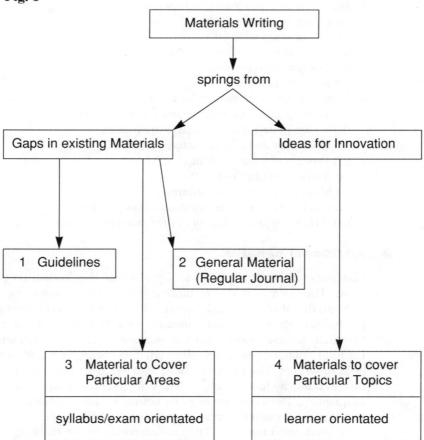

It will also be seen in Fig. 1 that there is a place, as well as for particular areas to be covered, for a medium for all materials produced, whether or not it is designed for a particular purpose. Some kind of regular newsletter or journal means that anything of value that has been successfully tried can have a wider distribution. Such material can then be incorporated into further publications. Under this heading too can come production of guidelines that can show the way to the kind of material needed.

Fig. 1 shows a possible framework. Actual examples from the Brunei project are as follows:

1 *Guidelines:*
   (a) Professional Aspects handbook, updated each year for the arrival of new teachers and covering all aspects of teaching in the country.
   (b) PCE exam analysis.
2 *General material:*
   (a) *Centre Well*: in-house journal, seventeen issues from March 1986 to May 1989. A total of 2,300 pages and 107 contributors. Material from here was widely used in (b).
   (b) Syllabus-based Resource Book: Worksheets and lesson plans to cover grammar part of English syllabus.
   (c) Subject booklets that provided material for use with Maths, Science, Geography and History syllabuses.
3 *Materials to cover particular areas:*
   (a) Listening comprehension
   (b) Information transfer
   (c) Serial story – 'Martin on Mars'
   (d) Composition pictures
   (e) Reading boxes
4 *Materials to cover particular topics:*
   (a) Topic packs – monsters, dinosaurs, colours
   (b) Video material from local programmes
   (c) Role-play and drama material
   (d) Process writing booklet
   (e) Stories for children
   (f) Making stories with children
   (a) – (c) were suggested by discussion groups.
   (d) – (f) were suggested by conference presentations.

## ■ Additional benefits

Materials writing has a far wider benefit than the production of materials alone. The rewards in this instance touch a wide variety of people.

First, the Ministry of Education. CFBT have passed copies of materials produced to the various departments of the Ministry of Education, and certain items to schools. This has increased their options in terms of sources for future material either by using what has been produced or by tapping the pool of writers. The materials have also led to workshops in schools and informal use by local teachers. The effectiveness of the benefits here are hard to quantify. The existence of more communicative material may make local teachers more open to future changes of methodology.

Second, local teachers. They now have access to teaching materials where few existed before, as well as contact with a different methodology and a different type of material from that used so far.

Third, the pupils. Such materials have given pupils a positive attitude towards English, which will affect future learning. Increased motivation and success have come from materials designed for them. Oral fluency has improved, and English is beginning to be seen as a useful tool rather than a school subject to be tolerated.

Fourth, the CFBT teachers. The amount of material produced has given them a rich resource, thus making teaching more rewarding. It has allowed all teachers to improve their teaching by trying out ideas and teaching techniques. As writers they have had the opportunity of practising the skills of writing and editing.

Fifth, the Centre itself. The greatest resource that CFBT has is its teachers. Materials writing by teachers produces professional teachers. The opportunities to participate in projects and see the results increase morale, and the productivity of the project. This in turn enhances the reputation of those involved as capable of producing a quality service in education.

## ■ Particular relevance to Primary teaching

I have so far described a number of the features of materials writing on the CFBT Primary project in Brunei. My main contention, that materials writing acts as a facilitator to the learning process, is true at any level, but it is particularly appropriate at Primary level for a number of reasons.

First, the younger the pupils, the more necessary it is that materials are close and familiar to them. This is not to say that there is no room for fantasy and imagination, but materials should reflect the commonplace in the child's surroundings which cannot be reproduced in commercial material. Second, confidence is crucial in effective language learning at the younger age level. The material must be at the right level, again something that cannot normally be achieved in commercial materials. Given that there are arguments for having a textbook, even a commercially produced one, there is at least a strong argument for plentiful resource or support materials developed locally.

At the stage of development of young learners, they have to be presented with stimuli and experiences around which language can be used. In any teaching situation some of these would be provided by teachers. Books are another excellent source of such stimuli, but these can be supplemented by using the artistic expertise of teachers. Pictures for both talking and writing, tape-recordings of noises, stories, conversations and realia are all an asset here. The use of songs, games and drama come under the same category. All these can be more appropriately designed by teachers on the spot. The guiding principle of successful Primary teaching in the UK has been child-centred learning. This principle applies equally to Primary EFL and supports the case for materials designed for specific groups.

## ■ Summary

This paper has described how on a particular project at Primary level, materials writing played an important part in many different ways in providing educational benefits to all concerned and in improving teaching and learning. It is not claimed that materials alone can effect change. However, it is right to conclude that, in any system, on any project, classroom teachers should be responsible for at least some of the materials writing, particularly at Primary level.

**Appendix 1:** Sample CFBT materials
# 1. Cue sheet for Primary 6. Item 135 by Janice Collins

1 <u>Example</u>

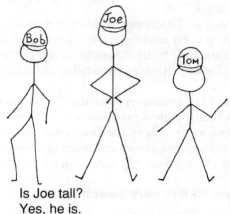

Is Joe tall?
Yes, he is.

Is he tall <u>enough</u> to pick the coconut?
No, he isn't tall enough to pick the coconut.

2.

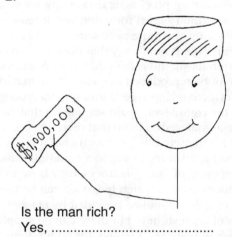

Is the man rich?
Yes, ...........................................

Is he rich <u>enough</u> to buy the ring?
No, he ...........................................

3.

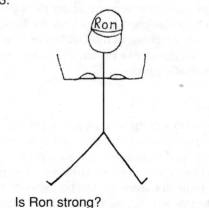

Is Ron strong?
...........................................

Is he strong <u>enough</u> to lift the weight?
...........................................

## 2. Sources of Light by Dee Dunstan

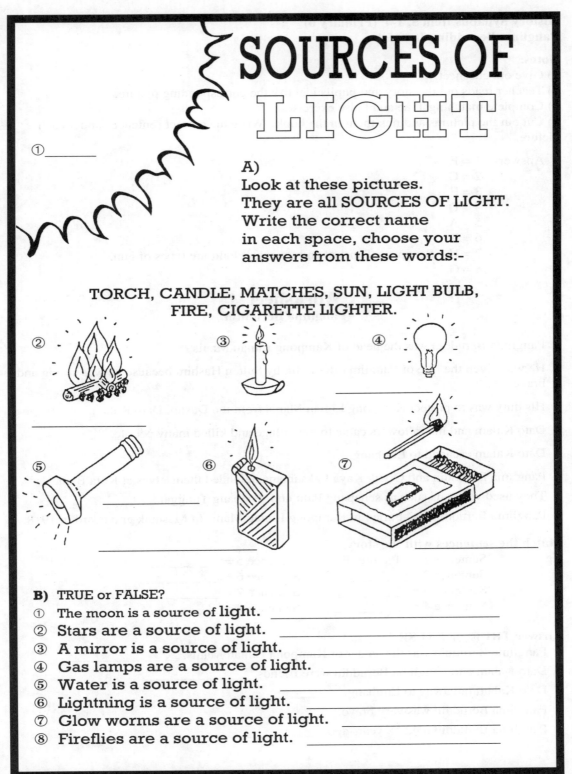

# SOURCES OF LIGHT

① _____

**A)**
Look at these pictures.
They are all SOURCES OF LIGHT.
Write the correct name
in each space, choose your
answers from these words:-

TORCH, CANDLE, MATCHES, SUN, LIGHT BULB,
FIRE, CIGARETTE LIGHTER.

② _____  ③ _____  ④ _____

⑤ _____  ⑥ _____  ⑦ _____

**B)** TRUE or FALSE?
① The moon is a source of light. _____
② Stars are a source of light. _____
③ A mirror is a source of light. _____
④ Gas lamps are a source of light. _____
⑤ Water is a source of light. _____
⑥ Lightning is a source of light. _____
⑦ Glow worms are a source of light. _____
⑧ Fireflies are a source of light. _____

107

## 3. **Panglima Beruddin** by Jenny Wade

**History Syllabus Item 5. 1-4  (Primary 6)**
**Panglima Beruddin** - Item 5.1

**Notes:**
1) Give out cuesheet.
2) Teacher reads out the story and pupils identify the corresponding picture.
3) Complete matching True and False exercises.
4) Cut out the pictures and tick them in the book.  Write the correct sentences under each picture.

```
Answers   1 = E
          2 = C
          3 = F
          4 = D
          5 = A
          6 = B
          7 = H    Senepang Tunggal and senepang Palit are types of gun.
          8 = G
```

# Worksheet  1
### Panglima Beruddin

1  Panglima Beruddin was the head of Kampong Limau Manis.

2  He was given the title of Panglima Beruddin by Sultan Hashim because he was strong and brave.

3  His duty was to protect Kampong Limau Manis from the Dusun, Dato Kalam.

4  Dato Kalam and his followers came to the village and killed many people.

5  Dato Kalam escaped to Limbang.

6  Panglima Beruddin and Orang Kaya Laksamana defended themselves at Kota Batu.

7  They used weapons such as senapang Palit and senapang Tunggal.

8  Panglima Beruddin was buried in Kampong Limau Manis in Masutak graveyard in 1918.

**Match the sentences with the story.**
e.g.        Sentence 1  =  Picture  E        Sentence 5 = _____
            Sentence 2 = _____        Sentence 6 = _____
            Sentence 3 = _____        Sentence 7 = _____
            Sentence 4 = _____        Sentence 8 = _____

**Answer TRUE  or FALSE**
1  Panglima Beruddin was the leader of Kampong Limau Manis. _____
2  Dato Kalam and Panglima Beruddin were friends. _____
3  Dato Kalam ran away to Limbang. _____
4  Panglima Beruddin was very brave. _____
5  Panglima Beruddin died 18 years ago. _____

# Panglima Beruddin Cue Sheet

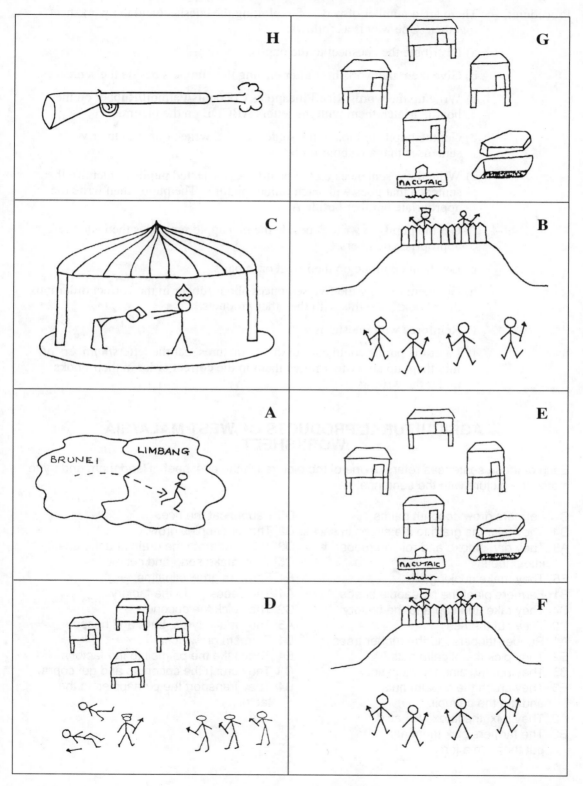

## 4. Agricultural Products of Malaysia by Hugh Leburn

Procedure:    There are a number of ways of exploiting the cuesheet and the worksheet together.  One way is as follows:

a) Distribute the cuesheet to the pupils.

b) Give them the worksheet after erasing the numbers beside the sentences.

c) Write up the words Rice/Pineapples/Coconuts/Palmoil/Rubber on the board.  Match them with the letters ABCDE on the pictures.

d) Get the pupils to look at the sentences and write A next to the rive sentences that are about rubber.

e) Write these sentences on the board.  Ask selected pupils to identify the sentence that goes with each rubber picture.  The pupils then write the appropriate number beside A.

f) Get the pupils to write B beside the pineapple sentences then add the appropriate numbers.

g) Let them continue on their own or in pairs.

h) Get them to copy the five sentences about rubber in the correct order into their books.  Do this with the other products.

i) Reinforce with questions.

j) Later the pupils could cut out the 25 pictures, cut the letters/numbers off, mix them up an try to arrange them in the correct order in their books under the writing.

## AGRICULTURAL PRODUCTS OF WEST MALAYSIA WORKSHEET

Each of these sentences refers to one of the pictures in the cuesheet.  Read them and try to match the picture with the sentence.

C1  Farmers grow coconut palms.
D4  They take the grain to the shops in sacks.
A3  They dry, smoke and roll the rubber into sheets.
E5  They make cooking-oil.
B1  Farmers plant the pineapple seeds.
C4  They take the copra to the factory.
D2  They cut the rice.
A1  Rubber-tappers tap the rubber trees.
E2  They pick the oilpalm nuts.
B5  They put the pineapples in tins.
E3  They crush the oilpalm nuts and get the palmoil.
A2  They mix the latex with acid.
B3  The farmers pick them and put them on a lorry.

D5  People eat the rice.
B2  The pineapples grow.
D3  They separate the grain and the chaff.
C5  They make soap and cosmetics.
E1  Farmers grow oilpalms.
A4  The seeds go to the factory.
C2  They pick the coconuts.
A5  They make tyres, balls and hoses.
D1  Farmers grow rice.
E4  They take the palmoil to the factory.
C3  They crush the coconuts and get copra.
B4  They transport the pineapples to the factory.

# Agricultural Products of West Malaysia
## Cuesheet

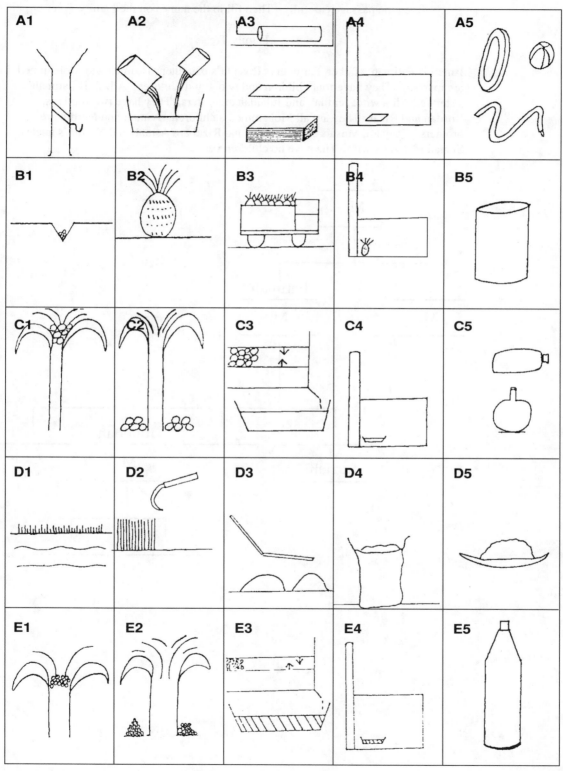

## 5. Family Tree by Jan Wells

Read the passage carefully.  Then fill in the names on the Family Tree:

Family Tree

Ismail is Fatimah's father. Fatimah is Rosnita's daughter.  Fatimah and Mohammed are married.  They have four children and two grand-children.  Alizah is Fatimah's sister and Ali's wife. Jemilah and Julaidah are sisters.  They have two brothers, Rosdan and Rizal.  They are all Mohammed's children.  Asmali and Nordin are brothers.  They are Musa's sons. Rosdan and Rizal are Asmali and Nordin's uncles. Suziah is Rizal's wife.  The have no children yet.

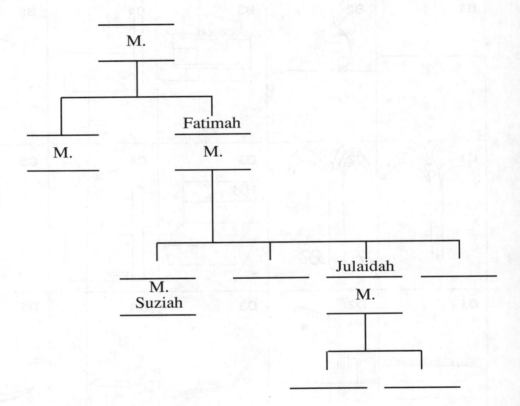

# 6. Mime to practice phrasal verbs by Eunice Stephen

| | |
|---|---|
| Put on three rings. | Put on a brooch. |
| Put on a watch. | Put on two rings. |
| Put on a bangle. | Put on three bangles. |
| Pick up a small, heavy box. **Then** put it down on your desk. | Pick up a small, light box. Then, put it down on the floor. |
| Pick up a big, heavy box. Then, put it down on your desk. | Pick up a big, light box. Then, put it down on the floor. |
| Pick up a butterfly. Then, put it down on your desk. Be careful! | Pick up two tiny beads. Then, put them down on your desk. |

### 7. The Old Man by David Blackwell

### Final Copy - Low Ability Pupils.

He is a man.  He is forty years old.
He is a grandfather.
He lives in Malaysia.
He likes nasi goreng.

### Final copy.  Average ability pupils.

This is a man.  He is an old man.
He is forty years old.
His name is Mr. Lemmen.
He lives in Europe.
He is a grandfather.
He has two ears.
His moustache is grey.

### Final copy - High ability pupils.

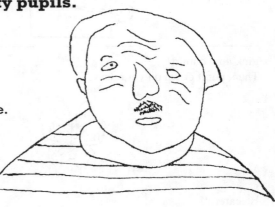

He is an old man.
He has a brown face.
His face is wrinkled.
He has white hair.
He has a big, grey moustache.
He has a big nose.
He has brown eyes.
He has a small mouth.
He is John's grandfather.

## 8. The Grandfather by Anne Graham

# Part 4

# Language in the classroom

## Introduction

What kind of language do classroom tasks demand? Do EFL textbooks reflect *children's* language? How can awareness of patterns of teacher–pupil interaction help our teaching? The papers in this Part raise these fundamental questions, and suggest different ways in which investigating the language of tasks, texts and teachers can help us explain children's learning in our classrooms.

Collaborative task-based learning figures in many young learner classrooms. However, teachers may not be aware of the strategies which pupil–pupil collaboration involves. Brewster's paper presents the findings of a study of young learners engaged in problem-solving and information-sharing tasks. She gives important insights into the different demands of the two types of task, and discusses ways in which children could be made aware of the strategies they use, and so be helped to take more control of their own learning. In this, she points to the importance of helping learners 'learn how to learn'. It is an idea which is receiving increasing attention in ELT (see Ellis and Sinclair, 1989) and Brewster suggests ways in which young learners too can be helped to prepare for learning tasks, plan their strategies and reflect on what they have done.

Hurst's paper looks at the language of textbook dialogues. Based on a study of British and Malaysian nine to fourteen-year olds, Hurst uses our socio-linguistic awareness of how we vary our language when with different people. She asked the children to comment on the dialogues in some textbooks, and also observed ways in which the children used language with each other. There were many differences between the language used by the children and that presented in the textbooks. Are we giving children a diet of adult functions and topics? She suggests that the children find the textbook dialogues unchildlike in many important ways, and she raises the question of whether this lack of perceived relevance might contribute to children's lack of enthusiasm for learning English. The paper suggests an area which classroom teachers can investigate in their own contexts, and points again to the critically important decisions about relevance which teachers have to make when deciding on what 'English' to teach.

Bloor's paper deals with a context which is very widespread, but not often studied (though see the papers in Parts 3 and 5). It is that of the 'chalk and talk' classroom, where resources other than the blackboard and teacher are few. Taking Kenyan primary classrooms as her base, Bloor focuses on teacher–pupil interaction in teacher to whole class modes. By examining points of breakdown in communication between teacher and pupils, Bloor seeks to present understandings of what helps effective use of language. She also makes some interesting suggestions about how both teachers and pupils could be helped to be more aware of ways of using English to achieve successful interaction. In this she points, in a whole-class context, to similar issues to those raised by Brewster. Specific strategies of interaction are utilised in whole-class teacher–pupil discourse. Can we profitably think about raising the awareness of both teachers and pupils of the strategies they use?

The three studies in this Part are suggestive of investigations which teachers might feel they could adapt for studying their own classrooms. Understanding how we use language in the classroom and the language demands we make on children, is a means of giving teachers more control of teaching. It can be a much needed source of increasing teacher-confidence and interest in what we do.

# *D*o *I have to do it from my mind?*
# *Interactional strategies in task-based*
# *groupwork*

## Jean Brewster

## ■ Introduction

In primary schools in Britain today there is a great deal of emphasis on task-based learning during which children collaborate to solve problems, make models, retell stories and so forth. The importance of social interaction for children's cognitive development has been highlighted primarily by Vygotsky (1978). He argued that cognition develops in the process of social interaction and that the provision of a social context for problem-solving forces children to formulate and express their ideas verbally. This encourages the child to move from spontaneous and unconscious problem-solving to one which is more self-directed and consciously monitored.

Vygotsky claimed that the provision of a social context for problem-solving elicited from children their otherwise implicit strategies. Many children possess the resources and underlying competences which enable them to collaborate with each other successfully. However, some educationalists would argue that teachers have an important role to play in teaching their learners the interactional skills required to work together in groups. Indeed, as early as 1975 the Bullock Report referred to the need for teachers' 'planned intervention' when setting up and monitoring groupwork. The crucial question that has remained relatively unanswered is what form such intervention might take in order to maximise the benefits which are held to accrue from learning in small groups.

The teacher's role in organising, monitoring and evaluating task-based collaborative learning is complex. To make this easier we need more indication of what it is that learners are or are not doing which leads to comparative success or lack of success in completing a task. We also need an understanding of the most effective strategies required to complete specific task types, such as persuading others, or problem-solving.

The findings outlined in this paper arise from an investigation of the interactional strategies used by ten-year old native-speakers working on different task types. These findings aim to illuminate teachers' understanding of some of the processes involved in group discussions. To this end the following three questions are posed, the answers to which might shed some light on the teacher's role in teaching children how to work together and to develop effective strategies for different task types. The first two questions are concerned with task types and the teaching of interactional skills, issues which are of importance in children's language development, whether they are native-speakers or learners of a foreign language. The third question sets out to highlight the similarities between these two sets of learners in terms of the support required for task-based learning.

1  Which types of task generate the most fruitful collaboration for language and learning purposes?
2  How far is it possible to distinguish between more and less effective interactional strategies and use this knowledge to improve children's interactional skills?
3  To what extent can the insights gained by studying the language used by native-speaker children be used to inform the teaching of bilingual learners?

## ■ Tasks and interactional strategies

Although task-based learning has in recent years become prominent in EFL teaching, the term 'task' is rarely defined since its meaning is generally assumed to be self-evident (but see Ur, 1981). This non-definition may have led to the concealment of differences between the interactional outcomes of tasks. In examining the notion of task, Ur (*op. cit.*) emphasises the requirement that it involve cognitive activity and give rise to very definite outcomes, suggesting:

> Each task should consist of a thinking process and its outcome in the form of a tangible result. It is not enough just to think out a problem or explore the ramifications of a conflict: the results must be written down, ticked off, listed, sketched or tape-recorded in some way. (p. 13)

Many materials for TEFL include task-based groupwork to provide free and guided practice for students. However, comparatively little research has been carried out to evaluate the kinds of language use which derive from different task types. One study by Pica and Doughty (1985) examined the extent to which task-based groupwork facilitated the language acquisition of bilingual learners. They found that the choice of task was crucial as many tasks did not compel individuals to negotiate meaning, a crucial stage in interaction. Many tasks simply invited learners to participate in a discussion. Pica and Doughty make reference in particular to commonly used decision-making tasks: 'these tasks did not place demands on students to (1) confirm or clarify each other's meaning or (2) check their mutual comprehensibility or (3) participate at all' (p. 246). The authors argue that tasks based upon an information gap, such as text-based jigsaw tasks or picture-based comparisons, require more negotiation and conversational adjustment, which, through providing more comprehensible input, leads to more effective language acquisition.

This is not to say that all collaborative tasks should be based on an information gap, but it is clear that the teacher's selection of appropriate tasks ought to be well informed. Tasks that are interesting, contextualised and purposeful, staged at the appropriate linguistic and cognitive level, have a clearly defined goal and allow participants to adopt a specific interactional role are most likely to succeed, both in terms of producing meaningful language and in ensuring that participants are supported in contributing to group discussions.

Another important factor in task-based interaction is the extent to which learners feel confident in tackling different kinds of task. Problems for learners frequently occur in three areas: firstly, there may be difficulties with the specification of the task, for example, understanding how a jigsaw task works. Secondly, problems may arise with expressing the ideas contained within the task, for example, retelling a story in order to help others complete a matching exercise. Finally there may be difficulties with understanding the text itself, for example, understanding the written or spoken version of the story in order to be able to retell it.

To help learners overcome some of these problems we need first of all to develop an understanding of the types of interactional strategy different tasks require. We can do this to some extent by placing ourselves in the role of the learner and predicting the likely language and strategies which the learners will use. Research can also help by analysing what it is that learners actually do. Detailed studies of children's collaborative interaction, such as those carried out by Barnes and Todd (1977), Phillips (1985), Renshaw and Garton (1986) and Brewster (1987), reveal particular patterns of interaction or discourse styles manifested by successful interactants. Teachers can then support less successful learners by encouraging or teaching them to use similar, more effective strategies.

To return to the notion of 'planned intervention', the teacher's role is to ensure that learners thoroughly understand the task requirements before they begin the task. Learner-training with models and task rehearsal, with the whole class or in small groups, using the target language entirely, or, more probably, using the L1, will be useful here. Children usually need visual and aural support of a text in order to understand it, along with rehearsal of some of the most important language for communicating their ideas. What has been ignored, both in teaching fluent English speakers and developing bilinguals, is teaching children how to co-operate and interact in groups.

## ■ Interactional strategies used in two tasks

The investigation outlined in this paper examined the strategies used by ten-year old native-speakers while working on two tasks. Both tasks contained an information gap which led to information sharing where at least one participant might be considered a 'primary knower'.

The first task was a jigsaw task based on the topic of 'Castles'. In this case, the children, having read different texts, worked in threes to help each other complete a matching exercise. Speaker A, for example, worked with two other speakers, neither of whom had read her text, to help them match pictures with labels based on this text. The second task took the well-trodden path of 'Following A Route', with the complication that the maps of the two participants (the 'explainer' and the 'follower') were not identical. I shall begin with the findings of the simpler 'Map' task.

## ■ Strategies used in following a route on a map

This task was worked on by four pairs who used strikingly different macro-strategies to deal with their difficulties when explaining and following the route. In two of the pairs the explainer simply retraced the route, sometimes three times, before establishing the fact that there were differences in their maps. The tacit assumption here appeared to be that the follower must have been at fault. By contrast, the follower in the third pair became impatient with his partner, took over the explainer's role and retraced the route himself, thus reversing the interactant roles. The fourth pair used neither of these strategies; the route was not retraced and after a short discussion the two participants shared information to resolve the difficulties they were having.

### Communicative stress and active followers

It is fair to say that the role of the follower was likely to give rise to feelings of 'communicative stress' since s/he was liable to feel that the problem lay in their lack of understanding rather than because there were problems with the maps; for this reason the analysis focuses on this role.

The most important factor appeared to be the difference in followers' perceptions of the nature and scope of their role. Using what might be called more 'assertive' strategies, some followers saw their role as very active, thereby contributing a great deal to the interaction and drawing upon a wide range of language. Other followers adopted a much more passive role, contributed less to the interaction and used a more limited range of language.

There were five successful strategies deployed by active followers:
(*Note:* $E$ = explainer, $F$ = follower.)

1 Providing feedback to show understanding, achieved either by repeating directions or responding to checks made by the explainers, e.g. $E$: Got that? ➜ $F$: Yeah.
2 Asking questions to clarify misunderstandings, e.g. $F$: Which one do I go up to?
3 Supplying information in order to gain control of the topic or to clarify misunderstandings, e.g. $F$: I go to Fieldside Road.
4 Disagreeing with or challenging the 'explainer', e.g. $E$: You turn right up to New Lane onto New Lane. ➜ $F$: No but that would mean turning left.
5 Giving directions to the 'explainer', e.g. $F$: Tell me what street I stop at.

Examples can be seen in the following extracts from the tapescript where $S$ is an 'active' follower.

### Extract 1
Strategies 2 and 3

> ➜ $S$: Right. Do I start from the beginning of that?
>
> $J$: Yeah.
>
> ➜ S: Yep. I go to Fieldside Road.
>
> $J$: Now you walk forward.
>
> ➜ $S$: Yeah. To Fieldside Road.

Generally $S$ asks numerous questions, predicts where he might be going and takes control of the route himself. In the next extract we see an example of a challenge with an explanation:

### Extract 2
Strategy 4

> *J*: You're just about to come onto Elm Lane. You take...
>
> →*S*: No. Cos you just told me to go down there. I was there before yeah? But then you told me to go back.

Finally, *S* becomes very impatient and asks several questions as well as giving a directive:

### Extract 3
Strategy 5

> →*S*: Where do I stop?
>
> *J*: No. Not all the way down. Not all the way down.
>
> →*S*: Yeah but you. Yeah but to where? To what?
>
> *J*: Look. There. There.
>
> →*S*: Tell me what street I stop at.

Here we can see that an 'assertive' follower takes an active part by constantly making use of the contextual information to identify inadequate instructions and to specify what additional information he needs.

#### Passive followers

In the second, more 'compliant' approach, the follower appeared more willing to accept the explainer's primary knower status, thereby remaining relatively passive and contributing little to the interaction. This usually meant that the differences between the maps were not fully established.

A good example of a more passive approach can be seen in the next extract where it became clear to the follower that the explainer was confused about how to give directions:

### Extract 4

> *A*: Which way is your left? Which way do you mean left?
>
> → *R*: No. I'm not telling you because then it will give it away.
>
> (pause)
>
> → (no comment from *A*)

It may be useful at this point to bear in mind that the data are based on native-speakers of similar ability, i.e. they are not learners of English. Here the failure of the follower to challenge the explainer's tactics can only be explained in two ways: either the follower does not perceive this as a useful strategy, although he would have the linguistic knowledge to formulate a challenge, or he is unwilling to use this strategy since he does not wish to challenge the authority of the so-called primary knower. If one child is overly compliant there are clearly going to be problems with this kind of task. Equally, if the other participant is unable or unwilling to see another's point of view it is unlikely to lead to successful collaboration.

To summarise, there were several qualitative differences in the strategies used. In less successful approaches to this task there were two types of inadequacy: the first was a failure on the part of the explainer to be specific and for the follower to challenge this. The second was the failure of the 'follower' to take an active part in the task when difficulties were perceived. Thus, even interactants who are fluent speakers of English are nevertheless individually differentiated in their ability to deploy effective interactional strategies. All the more need, therefore, for bilingual learners to have support provided in using specific interactional strategies. This can be achieved through direct instruction or modelling and awareness-raising.

## ■ Speaker types and group processes

We are all aware of the differences in the degree of co-operativeness shown by participants when working together. Participants may not wish or be able to interact co-operatively, perhaps because they have momentarily switched off, or because the cognitive demands of the task prevent them from fully co-operating. Other factors which may contribute to speakers' differing approaches to collaboration are provided by writers such as Zimmerman and West (1975), Ickes and Barnes (1978), Smith (1985), and Brewster (1987).

Smith (op. cit.) suggests that differences in patterns of interaction can be accounted for by setting up two main dimensions termed 'affiliation' and 'control'. The 'control' dimension, as described by Smith, 'orders people, situations and episodes in terms of the extent to which they provide the opportunity for exerting active control over the process and outcomes of interaction' (p. 135). We have already seen the ways in which 'active followers' on the 'Map' task were concerned to exert control over the process and thereby the outcomes of the task, and that active involvement was more likely to lead to success in the task than a more passive approach. The 'affiliation' dimension refers to a tendency to avoid such control in favour of strategies which elicit co-operation and support.

Brewster (*op. cit.*) analyses differences in group processes where speaker type and task type are the two main variables. She hypothesises that logic-based decision-making tasks tend to be more effectively completed if there is at least one speaker who is concerned to exert linguistic control by using tactics such as initiating topics, challenging others or giving and justifying opinions. By contrast, information-sharing tasks using an information gap tend to be more satisfactorily completed if speakers demonstrate a concern for supporting others. This is achieved by using strategies such as offering explanations when a speaker is in difficulty, or providing evidence for and agreeing with others' statements.

In practice, individual participants will not necessarily retain one or the other of these goals at all times. Speakers are likely to be influenced by the type of task on which they are working and by the behaviour of other members of their group. However, some speakers might be constrained by their own inflexibility and inability to adopt differing interactional strategies, regardless of the requirements of the task or the people with whom they are working. This may then lead to ineffective group discussions, such as decision-making tasks where no speaker is prepared to make a decision, or information-sharing tasks which are ruled by controlling rather than supporting strategies.

In order to tackle issues concerned with the social context of groups, teachers might like to consider the ways in which they choose children to work together and ways of raising children's awareness of what it means to collaborate in small groups. This issue will be considered in more detail in the final section. Before that, however, we turn to strategies used in a jigsaw task.

## ■ Effective strategies in a jigsaw task

In a jigsaw task we might predict that speakers concerned with the goal of co-operation and support would be most likely to share information and help each other effectively. Indeed, the findings reveal that the most effective groups were those in which speakers did not take a competitive attitude to participants' differing states of knowledge and were concerned to support each other. These groups deployed the following strategies when getting organised (subsumed under the heading 'Task management') and in completing the details of the task itself (see 'Task content').

### Task management

1  Co-operating to work out the task procedure by constant reference to the written instructions.
2  Checking that everyone in the group has understood the procedure and has the correct materials.
3  Working independently wherever possible, rather than immediately asking for the teacher's assistance.
4  Monitoring one's own and the group's understanding of the procedure so that stages in the task can be recognised.

### Task content

5  Monitoring one's own understanding, by admitting to a lack of understanding, for example, so that difficulties can be shared and explanations offered by other speakers.
6  Co-operating to share information by supplying details, asking questions or making suggestions.
7  Avoiding using competitive tactics, such as taunting others when they show a lack of knowledge or understanding.

Examples of effective task management can be seen in extracts from the tapescript:

### Extract 5
Strategies 1 and 2

> *R*:  Yeah, I've got it. C'mon. Open them up. There's these sentences and words and there's pictures. So you've got to match them up and you've got to help.

**Extract 6**
Strategy 3

> *R* Well let's ask Miss erm what { they
> → *L*:                              { No. Don't do that. Think.

**Extract 7**
Strategy 4

> *L*:  Done that part. Now what do we do? Where's the instruction card?

Like the 'Map' task, the jigsaw task also included an element of communicative stress. This stress was increased by those groups who introduced a competitive element into the interaction but was reduced by speakers who made most use of strategies 1–7. One group in particular seemed especially prepared to support each other by admitting to their own lack of understanding, failing to taunt others when they did not understand, and explaining details to each other. Examples can be seen below:

**Extract 8**  One 'expert' is explaining her text to the other two speakers so that they can match pictures to text.

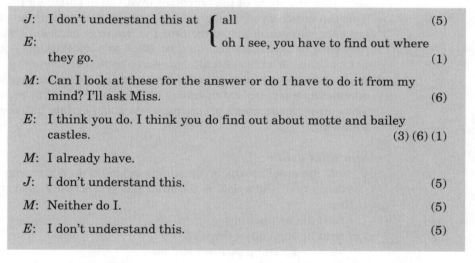

> *J*:  I don't understand this at { all                                    (5)
> *E*:                              { oh I see, you have to find out where
>       they go.                                                            (1)
>
> *M*:  Can I look at these for the answer or do I have to do it from my
>       mind? I'll ask Miss.                                                (6)
>
> *E*:  I think you do. I think you do find out about motte and bailey
>       castles.                                                     (3) (6) (1)
>
> *M*:  I already have.
>
> *J*:  I don't understand this.                                            (5)
>
> *M*:  Neither do I.                                                       (5)
>
> *E*:  I don't understand this.                                            (5)

As we can see, all three participants admitted that they did not fully understand how to complete the task. They therefore turned to the texts and the instructions, asked questions, made suggestions and shared information to help each other. This stood in contrast to other groups who were much more competitive, did not admit having difficulties, failed to refer to the task instructions and taunted others who seemed to hesitate. Other unsuccessful strategies included a failure to ask questions or to check details when an unhelpful message was given. There may be several reasons for this; one is that certain learners may not have the confidence to challenge an inadequate message. Another is the justified reluctance certain learners show in displaying assumed ignorance to others who taunted them. Certain speakers, including the participant who had been a successful 'active' follower in the 'Map' task, seemed very uncertain of how to put aside individual concerns when working with others to achieve a co-operative goal.

## ■ Conclusions and implications

There are at least three implications which arise from the discussion of interactional strategies described thus far. They concern the need for teachers to:

1  raise their own awareness of group processes.
2  raise children's awareness of interactional and learning strategies for task-based collaboration.
3  carefully consider the above in selecting or designing suitable tasks for groupwork.

### Raising teachers' awareness

The first implication concerns the need in teacher training, both initial and in-service, to raise teachers' awareness of what language use occurs in group discussions. This requires an understanding of task types and their discourse outcomes and some of the processes involved in collaborating with others. This can be achieved through ensuring that teachers work on collaborative tasks themselves, noting at the time the language and interactional strategies they need to use. Teachers could be asked to work through a questionnaire or tick columns in a checklist after working on two different task types. They might, for example, compare the language and strategies used after completing a picture/text matching activity or sequencing events in a story. The questionnaire might group questions under certain headings, such as the following:

### Strategies used

1  Note the order in which you completed the task. For example, what did you do first? Put a tick by the strategies you actually used and then order them.
    • read the instructions.
    • read through all of the text.
    • started matching pictures and text.
    • started sequencing the text.
    • started sequencing the pictures, etc.
2  Did anyone in the group:
    • explain the instructions to someone?
    • ask someone else's opinion?
    • provide evidence for their own or someone else's opinion?
    • disagree with someone else?
    • say that they did not understand something? etc.

Were these strategies useful to the discussion?

### Language used

3  Which vocabulary did you need to read/understand?
   Which vocabulary did you need to use?

4  Which sentence patterns did you find yourself repeating?
   e.g.This goes first because ...
        I think this one is after/before this one.
        This one belongs here so this one's next, etc.

5  Which of the following language functions do they represent?
   e.g.describing details, sequencing events using first, then, etc., giving
        opinions, giving reasons using because, making inferences using so,
        etc.

6  Using your answers to the above, work out the kind of language and
   strategies a specified group of learners would need when completing
   similar tasks. How much of this would be new language? How many of
   the strategies could be transferred to other tasks?

### Raising children's awareness

Recently a great deal of interest has developed in learner-training, that is,
learning to manage the learning process by being able to bring one's mental
processes under conscious scrutiny and thus more effectively under control.
It may seem that, however desirable this may be, it is beyond the capacity of
primary school children. However, recent studies, such as those described by
Nesbit and Shucksmith (1986), show that this may not be the case. They cite
research by Robinson and Robinson (1982) which showed that even four and
five-year olds could be trained to use task-specific strategies to enhance their
performance. All of the children in the study were given practice in listening
and speaking in small groups with the experimenter modelling the
appropriate behaviour. In addition, half of the children were also given
guidance about when and why listeners understood or failed to understand
them. All of the children showed improvements in how they performed and
understood, but the group receiving guidance improved much more than
those who only had practice. Nesbit and Shucksmith (*op. cit.*) go on to write:

> There is evidence that by the age of nine children have a store of
> metacognitive knowledge about how to cope with learning tasks but it is
> unreflecting knowledge and it is generally inadequately applied in
> transfer situations. (p. 72)

They argue that teachers have an important role in encouraging children to
reflect on the process of the learning they do, in preference to concentrating
solely on the product of learning. This is achieved by discussion of three
stages: preparing, planning and reflecting. In the first stage teachers can
explain what the goals of the exercise are and how they relate to previous
work. Once teachers have become skilled at predicting the most useful
language and strategies for different tasks, they can support their learners in
the planning stage by teaching the appropriate strategies and language
required for different task types. Nesbit and Shucksmith comment that
'children have problems diagnosing task types, and problems matching the
assigned task with any of their library of strategies or techniques' (p. 43).

With EFL learners, teachers can help children do this in the mother-tongue through discussion of the strategies and by asking the children to decide which of the strategies they might use or the sequence in which they might use them. These could be presented visually in the form of one or two picture flow-charts of strategies to be used. After completing the task, the groups compare the strategies they actually used. The effectiveness or otherwise of different kinds of strategy might then be discussed and modelled. It must be remembered, however, that modelling is more than demonstration or mere 'show and copy', and should represent an attempt to foster a transition for the child from control and direction to self-regulation. Interesting work has recently used the modelling process in the teaching of writing to children (see Graves, 1983). Nesbit and Shucksmith refer to studies which showed that 'successful' teachers were those who tended to use learning strategies themselves and demonstrated them to their pupils in their methodology.

Developing this kind of metacognitive awareness takes time; teachers of English may not feel it is their place to take responsibility for such work or feel that they have the time to do it. However, it would appear from several studies that this kind of training is time well spent since it is generally transferable to the children's other school work, whether in English or in their first language. Ideally, teachers of English would then be able to liaise with their colleagues to relate and reinforce the kind of awareness-raising the children were receiving in their other lessons to their lessons in English.

It is important that teachers of young learners ensure that their pupils not only understand the specification of the task and so forth, but begin to learn a range of strategies required to negotiate meaning in English for providing feedback to show they have understood something, indicating that they do not understand something, asking questions to clarify misunderstandings, or checking details when a message is inadequate. In addition to being taught explicitly beforehand, it might be possible to ask the children afterwards what they needed to say in English but only knew in their mother-tongue. Ideally, this kind of metacognitive awareness would be transferable to the children's other school work, whether in English or their first language.

With older primary schoolchildren, teachers might consider training their learners to work independently when following written instructions. This training might consist of the teaching of key vocabulary items, asking pupils to underline key instruction words, sequence instructions and to write instructions for other children to follow. Learners will then be supported in understanding instructions which ask them to sort (classify), put things in order (sequence), match (compare), say which is important (rank), and so forth.

In the final stage the children could be encouraged to reflect, by means of self or peer assessment tasks, on the learning that did or did not go on in their group and the possible reasons why. This could be achieved through sophisticated means, such as tape-recording, or more simply through learner diaries, group and individual questionnaires and so forth. An example of a questionnaire is given on page 129:

1   Today I think our groupwork was

    very good / not so good / bad


2   This was because

    — we liked / didn't like the work

    — we only talked about the work / we wasted time

    — we did / didn't understand what we were doing

    — we did / didn't help each other

    — we argued / didn't argue a lot


3   I think I talked

    — more / less than the others

    — about the same as the others


4   This was because

    — I was / was not interested

    — I knew / didn't know what to do

    — the others listened / didn't listen to me


5   Who was good at doing these things?

    — knowing what to do next

    — making people agree with him / her

    — explaining things

    — asking useful questions

      etc.


6   How did they do this?

    etc.

## Choosing tasks

The third implication concerns the types of task given to children. Where genuine collaboration does occur in primary classrooms, many teachers seem to emphasise logical problem-solving tasks where it is relatively easy to have one speaker in the group dominating the others. It requires a little thought to first of all work out the appropriate composition of groups and then to establish ways of ensuring that more than one child has a role in the group.

This can be achieved in larger groups by allocating specific roles, such as secretary or checker, or in pairs by ensuring, for example, that access to the task materials is easy for both participants and that writing tasks are shared and not dominated by one child. Finally, it is important that teachers consider carefully the repertoire of task types given to children to ensure that competitiveness does not take precedence over the development of children's ability to genuinely share information and co-operate.

# *Teaching children adult language*

## Rosalyn Hurst

In recent years there has been a considerable reawakening of interest in the teaching of English to pupils in the middle school age range, that is, starting at nine years. Programmes with continuity from this age to tertiary level have been established in countries with different language policies such as Malaysia and Portugal. But in these and other countries, despite the initial enthusiasms of teaching English to young learners, there is a significant drop-out of able pupils, particularly after two or three years of language learning. The reason for this apparent failure may lie not with teaching but within the language that is being taught.

The question I should like to pose is whether the school syllabus reflects *child* language needs and *child* usage. Many core syllabuses appear at first sight to adopt communicative principles which are attractive to young learners who are at a stage where they are more articulate than literate. However, these syllabuses are frequently adaptations of those designed for adults, many of which are based on analyses of adult needs undertaken by the Council of Europe, and Munby's analysis. Although adult textbooks, operating in a fiercely competitive market, have been altered to take into account changing adult language, the same is not apparent in school books. Thus the initial enthusiasm for second language learning is quickly replaced by a sense of alienation by the learner, and a disbelief in the language and activities of the characters in the textbooks.

A small study was conducted with a group of British and Malaysian school children in the age range nine to fourteen years, to attempt to identify the difficulties they face in second language programmes. The information from the British children was also used to uncover what recent moves there have been in English which have been adopted by young people, and this was contrasted with the expectations of learners from other cultures. The study has also been used in discussion with learners from other countries where English is taught to this age group.

### ■ Language functions

The communicative syllabus is centred on the use of language, thus the selection of function is critical to the learner. In adult courses the function of greeting is highly marked, because adults not only frequently meet strangers (and many of these strangers are indeed the motivation for learning a second language) but adults will greet acquaintances in a ritualised manner. This, it is argued, gives them time to weigh each other up, to work out status relationships or degree of friendliness. Even adults who know each other well and meet frequently adopt a greeting format, even when they are just in passing. For example:

Hallo.

Hallo. How are you?

Fine thanks and you?

Very well, see you soon.

Yes, bye.

This exchange carries a cultural expectation of recognition and may act as an indicator as to whether further communication is expected. Adults learn to recognise mood, so that if one is superior to the other, for example the boss, a warning might go out to colleagues, 'Watch out, the boss is in a bad mood this morning.'

Children, however, do not meet strangers alone. When a child is introduced to an adult he has not met before, another adult acts as an agent. For example, a child is introduced to a relation for the first time. The usual reaction of the child is to stare silently, unless prompted: 'Say hallo to your Uncle Jim.'

The children I interviewed claimed they did not greet friends, except for a casual 'Hi'. They did greet adults, but always in response to the adult, never initiating the interaction. Observing children entering school in the morning confirmed this. Most children just went and stood near their friends or just joined in a game. Most 'greetings' were non-verbal, a friendly shove in many cases. When there was conversation, it began immediately with 'Did you see ...?' and 'Look what I've got' and so on.

But in the school textbooks, children greet each other formally and in the adult manner. For example:

*Tina:* Hallo Tony. How are you today?

*Tony:* I'm fine thanks. How are you?

*Tina:* Fine. Thanks.

*Tim:* You're a good singer Tony. I like that song ... etc.

(Byrne and Palmer, 1982, *Track 1*)

When this dialogue was shown to British children, they thought that the participants must be adults. But the picture accompanying the text shows two teenagers talking. The British children immediately commented that there must be 'something wrong with Tony', they could not understand why such language was being used. They considered whether the participants were being ironic or even comic.

This highlights one of the major obstacles to syllabus design. It is that children do not accept the illocutionary force of some of the language or functions which they are being taught. Even when working in a second language, they appear to have an intuitive sense of what language is appropriate between children and what is purely imitative of adult behaviour.

The functions which operate in the child world are often more concerned with the side of school that adults do not see. It is essential to know, for example, the nicknames of teachers, the unwritten rules about where children of certain classes or groups of friends may play in the playground, the secret codes and messages that are passed between friends. Language among children is not always used to communicate to everybody; more often it is structured to be available to a few. It would be problematic to reflect this in a coursebook, although it is now a common feature of children's literature.

## ■ Province

Both the British and Malaysian children observed that they used different forms in their L1, depending on whether they were in the school playground with their friends, or at home. Sometimes this was a choice of accent. In the playground the dominant local accent rules regardless of whether parents or teachers view it as being desirable or not. The use of dialectical grammar deviations from the standard signals friendliness and informality among peers. Thus in the south of England, 'he ain't' and 'she goes' is more common in the playgrounds than the standard form of 'he isn't' and 'she says'.

In the school texts, however, no such deviation is found. Although it is argued that learners should not have to learn dialectical forms, the characters lose all credibility when using highly formal speech in supposedly informal gatherings of peers. In real life young learners are constantly being corrected, not only in their second but also their first language. They develop an awareness of alternative or more sophisticated forms of expression. While in the company of adults, teachers and parents, for example, children will use more standard forms, but peer group solidarity is marked by informality. In the textbook, however, formality rules, no matter what the context. For example, the dialogue below is between teenagers meeting outside a cinema:

| | |
|---|---|
| *Bosede:* | Hallo Maboudi. Where's Bola? |
| *Maboudi:* | I don't know. He asked me to meet him here. |
| *Hajo:* | He told us to be here at ten to nine. |
| *Maboudi:* | Perhaps he's got a lot of work at the hospital. Yesterday he had to stay there until nine o'clock. |
| *Hajo:* | Well, it's nearly nine o'clock now. If he doesn't come soon, we'll have to go in without him. |
| *Bosede:* | Yes, there's a good film on this evening. We mustn't miss the beginning. (Mills *et al*, 1971, *English for French Speaking Africa,* 5e) |

The speech is highly formal. Again, without an accompanying picture, it might be assumed that the interlocutors were adults, maybe only casual acquaintances, as the greater the social distance, the more formal the style (Cunningsworth, 1987). Teenagers would make some comment in either exasperation or in good humour on the delay of their friend. Nothing is said to mark the relationships within the group, and so the overall significance of the exchange is not communicated to young learners who cannot identify with such language in this context. Thus the variables which match the physical situation to the participants' roles appear in the dialogue to be contradictory when viewed from the experience and expectation of the learner.

There is an added difficulty with some English language textbooks designed for use in a particular country. The characters of the textbook appear to be nationals of that country. They discuss with each other how to buy something from the local shop, or the best way of travelling to the capital. While the youngest learners accepted this without question, the thirteen and fourteen-year olds could not understand why they have to undergo the work involved in learning a second language in order to discuss with others from their own country, with whom they share a first language, a topic about which they have shared information.

## ■ Status

The children interviewed were very conscious of status. Status normally comes with age. Whereas a difference of two years may be of no significance to an adult, children see it as an immense gap. Part of the privilege of being older is the ability to dominate. The children interviewed were asked about making requests. An older child said, 'If someone younger than me has my football, I just go and take it', so: no verbal communication. A younger child said, 'When the older ones have got my football, I say, give me my football, when I don't know them I might say please.' The British group thought that 'Would you mind giving me my football' was extremely threatening. Thus the rank of polite requests from formal to informal in adult language texts does not appear to apply to the child world.

All the children commented on the apparent absence of hierarchy or status positions among characters in books. In the dialogue below such status is not marked, despite the picture and the book story line showing children of differing ages:

> When's your birthday Kate?
>
> In May.
>
> Mine's in November.
>
> It's Chris' and Sam's birthday on Saturday. I'm giving Sam an astronaut.
>
> Oh no! I'm giving him an astronaut too.
>
> Astronauts! Oh dear, I'm giving them both astronauts. Look here they are.
>
> Gosh they're all the same. Four astronauts.
>
> (Johnson, 1983, *Now for English 1*)

It is impossible to tell from this dialogue which is the older child, or which child is the more dominant. In fact the dialogue is more appropriate for adult communication, for although one child has for some reason bought two presents and her friends comment 'Good old Sally', the fun and teasing element which would normally come from this conversation is missing. Normally children would react far more if they found they had all bought the same presents. Here there appears to be little surprise, no 'put down'.

In all the books surveyed there was no hierarchical structure among the characters. The textbook children were always polite and always negotiated activities. In adult coursebooks a strong story line, occasionally with dubious characters (for example, Lucky and George in *Kernel One*) does give interest and contrast, although teachers do not necessarily expect students to adopt criminal behaviour as a result. In other courses, characters make suggestions that are challenged or disagreed with, emotions are often expressed and then agreement reached. But the courses for young learners seem bland in comparison. Lessons might be taken from children's writers such as Roald Dahl.

## ■ Gender

Children of the age group nine to fourteen years are very conscious of gender. They are at the physical stages of puberty and adolescence. Although Malaysian and British societies have many differences in expected behaviour, both groups of children identified common differences in speech between boys and girls. Girls observed that boys talked more 'roughly'. This does not mean that boys swear, but that boys use more direct language, and use more dialectical forms. They also speak more loudly. One group observed that boys always stood differently from girls, and used more body movements, facial expression, a shift of the shoulder for example. Boys commented that their language was often corrected, and that boys together did not speak the same way as when girls were around. The girls interviewed claimed they had their own values. Some were very aware that to achieve at school they should not let themselves be dominated in class or outside school. Although they would rarely try to 'outshout' the boys, they apparently supported each other more, so that if someone was not getting attention from a teacher either her friends would call the teacher's attention, or they would help her with the problem. Girls in the survey not only read more than the boys, but read very widely, from pop magazines to those produced for the adult market, and from story books to literature.

No gender differences appeared in the textbooks examined. If the names were omitted from dialogues, it was impossible to tell which characters were male or female. Not only is the language indistinguishable between boys and girls, but so is the gender culture. They appear to take part in the same activities. There is no sparring or comment between them; everyone's role is unquestioned.

For this age group it is argued that omission of gender difference in language is a major reason for fourteen-year old boys dropping out of language classes. The boys interviewed in this age group thought the boys in the books were 'soft, a bunch of sissies, who talked like girls'. Such derisory comments may not be wholly accurate, but they identify the issue that the language being taught is not seen as being a desirable form to adopt.

## ■ Topic

The choice of topic is frequently far from being child-centred and it is therefore difficult for the young learner to relate to it. Sometimes the dialogues in the coursebooks involve children discussing the weather in abstract terms (something British adults do as part of phatic communication) or, as part of the Malaysian syllabus, offering condolences upon the death of a parent. Learners are often involved in adult-type interviews such as this:

Where are you from?

I'm from Japan.

How long are you here?

For a month.

What's your job?

I'm a factory manager.

Are you visiting a factory here?

Yes, in Newcastle.

I hope you have a good trip.

Thank you.

Goodbye.

Goodbye.

Topics are uncontroversial. The activities which give scope for communication are centred more on the games or quizzes which appear in some books, but communication is rarely stimulated by the dialogues.

What are young people interested in? Visiting a school in Thailand recently, a teacher introduced me to her class, whose English, she said, was very poor. As often occurs, the visitor was met with silence, until one boy asked 'Do you know Liverpool?' I assumed this meant the team, not the city, and a lively discussion began on the last game shown on the local television. The teacher was surprised at their knowledge of names, the positions of players and the team's previous results. So, like adults, motivation comes from saying what interests us. The British children rated sport highly; both British and Malaysian young learners were well informed about international developments and were in particularly interested in young people in other countries. Many belonged to clubs and community groups, which often faced difficulties with the local community, for example in finding funding for their activities, or finding meeting places. All children admitted that they spent quite some time just gossiping about their friends.

### ■ Lexis

Language is always moving on; there is constant change. It could be argued that many of the elements of changes later to be adopted into Standard English emerge with this age group. They seek to impress their individuality on the language. In all the language groups interviewed, the older generation commented on the new words, the new usage of language adopted by the younger people. Such changes are rarely positively accepted. However, such variation marks generations. For example, where once popular records appeared in the 'hit parade', they now appear in the 'charts'; where once a very good party, or a fast car might be 'fabulous', now it's 'wicked', as in 'That's a wicked car!'. Instead of 'I am very pleased with your present', the reintroduction of an older form of English is found among young people: 'I'm well pleased ...'

One of the delights of using such language is that it marks young people from the older generation. Nothing appeared to please both British and Malaysian children more than the comment, 'I cannot understand what you are saying.' from parents and teachers. Yet in the textbooks there is perfect harmony between generations. The fun, the element of playing with language, the international language of the young is missing.

### ■ The argument

Up to this point only the view of the young learner has been considered. What is the reaction of teachers? Although a comprehensive survey was not undertaken as part of this research, teachers are cautious about 'new' language. There is rightly the feeling that school books cannot be changed as often as those published for the international adult market. There is also the concern that if children are exposed to language other than the standard form, the learners may adopt it and be disadvantaged in examination or adult life. Finally, sudden change is outside the control of the teacher, for the teacher's own command of the target language may be dated but is 'correct', particularly in terms of national examinations. As Hutchinson (1987) points out, teachers are concerned about what they believe language learning to be about and not always about the learners' views.

However, it is becoming more economically viable to publish new editions of school books, and desktop publishing has resulted in supplementary materials of high quality being produced by teachers either in schools or regional teachers' centres. That children adopt, when speaking to peers, forms other than the recognised standard form, is seen now as being more appropriate in examinations of communicative competence than the consistent use of the formal mode. But the important factor is that the second language would be used, and not resisted or abandoned by the young learner at the first opportunity possible.

## ■ Conclusion

The survey indicated that young learners start the learning of a second language with much enthusiasm. The first steps at identifying yourself and friends, counting and telling the time are seen as useful activities. However, very often just when the syllabus demands more effort, more things to remember, the language becomes distant and not reflective of learner needs. If the syllabus is designed with actual and contemporary language for this group of learners, it may give the foundation for interested and interesting learning which may later be adapted and amended when adult life brings other language needs.

## Acknowledgement

The extract on page 136 is from *Enjoy Learning English 5*, a secondary course for francophone pupils. *English for French-Speaking Africa*, copyright Longman France 1986, reprinted with kind permission.

# Communication in the primary classroom

## Meriel Bloor

### ■ Introduction

In recent years there has been an increasing interest in developing the spoken language skills of young learners. Many methodological proposals have demanded more and more spontaneous spoken interaction between teacher and learners and between the learners themselves; and yet it seems that we really know very little, except at some kind of intuitive level, about how far non-native speaker children *are able* to enter into interaction in English at different stages of their development.

In spite of the increase in research into classroom teaching and learning over the past decade (see Chaudron, 1988, for an overview), very little research has been done into what problems arise in classroom interaction or into how experienced teachers encourage successful communication.[1] There must, of course, be a wealth of experience in teachers' heads, but it is very difficult to capitalise on such experience in teacher training.

In his book *Observation in the Language Classroom* (1988) Allwright makes a plea for more *systematic* observation in the language classroom. He explains that this means 'keeping a record of classroom events in such a way that it can be later studied, either for teacher training or for research purposes'. He also makes the point that recordings themselves, although interesting, are not in themselves enough. The significant things that happen in the classroom (the classroom 'data', as linguists call it) have to be analysed by procedures that are made explicit since it is only in this way that teachers can critically interpret the findings and make use of them effectively.

What I attempt to do here is to report on some research into the use of language in classrooms and to propose tentative implications for teacher training. I am indebted to the work of Charles Oduol (1987), who recorded about sixty hours of classroom interaction in Kenyan primary classrooms, which he used as the basis for his research for a doctoral degree. This was a study of the ways in which primary teachers overcome communication problems during the changeover period from Kiswahili to English-medium teaching that takes place in the fourth year of primary school. It is mainly data from his recorded corpus that I use for the examples in this paper.

### ■ The classroom setting

Every classroom is different, and any classroom varies from day to day and from lesson to lesson. The Kenyan primary classroom is no exception. However, there are certain features that the classrooms discussed here have in common.

Most children in these classrooms come from Kikuyu speaking families although a number of other first languages are represented too. All the children have learned Kiswahili as a second language and used it for the first three years of schooling. English is their third (and in some cases fourth) language.

In spite of this multilingual setting, the recordings show that for the most part the lessons are conducted in English, as is official education policy, but, not surprisingly, some teachers resort to Kiswahili from time to time.

## ■ An observational framework

In order to help give a general picture of the way language is used in these classes, I will first describe what the recordings reveal about the purposes and means of communication. To do this, I have used a set of questions taken from Fanselow (1977).

Fanselow attempted to set up a system for observing and recording different types of communication in the language classroom. He established five headings, in the form of questions.

1  Who communicates (with whom)?
2  What is the pedagogical purpose of the communication?
3  What mediums are used to communicate content?
4  How are the mediums used?
5  What areas of content are communicated?

These questions, with the possible exception of Question 4, are very useful as a starting point if we wish to consider how we as teachers use language in lessons. Question 4, 'How are the mediums used?' requires very complex linguistic answers that are not relevant to the main issues of this paper, so it is not discussed further here.

For any aspect of a lesson there is a wide range of potential answers to the questions posed by Fanselow. However, if we apply this observational framework to the Kenyan lessons, we find that the range of answers is strictly limited. Thus, for example, we find no instances of communication between learners in groups since the lessons in question did not require groupwork. Moreover, there are very few instances of English used to express questions to which the teacher did not already know the answer. 'Real' questions (what Brock, 1986, called 'referential questions') are rare. There are plenty of 'testing' questions (what Stubbs, 1983, also called 'pseudo questions'), but questions asking for information that the teacher does not already possess or for learners' attitudes or opinions, such as we would expect to find from time to time in so-called 'communicative' classrooms, are not normal in the lessons in question.

Such features are no doubt partly a reflection of the shortage of books and other teaching materials and partly a result of the chosen teaching style. In Oduol's words, teachers 'rely mainly on the chalk and talk method of teaching'.

### Who communicates?

Thus, in relation to the question 'Who communicates?' although Fanselow identifies the four possible participant groups of *the teacher, the individual student, a group of students, the class* (which implies a wide variety of possible lines of communication), the Kenyan classes contain mainly instances of the teacher addressing the whole class and the children responding to the teacher in chorus. This can be represented as follows:

Teacher —— whole class

The only other common lines of communication are between the teacher and an individual nominated student:

> Teacher —— individual student

## What is the purpose of the communication?

Fanselow's question about the 'pedagogical purpose' of the communicative act is concerned with *interactional purpose*, that is to say with the reason why each utterance takes place. Teachers and pupils produce utterances for a variety of reasons and we can describe these in more or less detail. Fanselow's four main purposes are:

1  to structure (prepare and organise classroom activities).
2  to solicit (ask questions and set tasks).
3  to respond (perform tasks or answer questions).
4  to react (perform verbal acts that are not requested).

Each of these purposes appears in the lessons, but most characteristic and by far the most common purposes are *solicit* and *respond*. Repeatedly the teacher asks questions of the class and expects spoken answers. Incidentally, this type of exchange was identified by Sinclair and Coulthard (1975, p. 48) and Stubbs (1983, p. 29) as characteristic of much formal teaching in Britain, but whereas in native-speaker classrooms the response is normally followed by some feedback from the teacher ('Good', 'That's right', and so on), in Kenya the feedback often seems to be omitted.

What Fanselow calls 'respond' includes non-verbal responses, like nodding to signify 'yes', or opening a book in response to the teacher's instruction, as well as spoken responses. However, it is spoken responses (or the failure to produce appropriate responses) that are of interest here. Therefore, following Sinclair and Coulthard, and Stubbs, I prefer to use the more precise terms:

> Elicitation —— response

*Elicitation*, roughly the equivalent of *solicit*, is Sinclair and Coulthard's (1975, p. 28) more precise term for an 'act the function of which is to request a linguistic response', which is exactly the function of the teacher initiations considered in this analysis. *Response* is likewise similar to *respond* but it excludes non-verbal responses which Sinclair and Coulthard deal with as a separate category of act.

## What mediums are used?

With respect to the question 'What mediums are used?', Fanselow identifies a lengthy set of potential mediums classified into the three groups:

> Linguistic        Non-linguistic        Para-linguistic

*Linguistic* covers everything that incorporates verbal messages, spoken or written, *Non-linguistic* incorporates video, pictures, film, and other codes, and *Para-linguistic* includes physical movement, facial expression, and so on. With the exception of the use of pictures and the occasional use of a blackboard or written exercise, the mediums used in Oduol's corpus are:

Linguistic: Aural (spoken language), and

Para-linguistic (gestures and occasionally special stress)

In the bilingual classroom, an important factor in the issue of *medium* is the choice of language. In the Kenyan data, some (but not all) of the teachers choose to switch from English to Kiswahili at what we might call *stress points* in the discourse. For example, in Extract 1 the teacher (*T*) switches language and gives the same elicitation in Kiswahili at a point when it appears that the pupil (*P*) does not understand the elicitation in English.

### Extract 1

*T*: Okay. Can you give me a number?

*P*: [No response]

*T*: Tell me any number that you know of.

*P*: [No response]

*T*: *Niambieni 'nambari' fulani kutoka kwa kichwa. 'Nambari' yoyote. Nereah.*

*P*: Eight.

It is, therefore, important, not only to discover how the teacher communicates, but also to consider which language is in use at any given time.

## What areas of content are communicated?

In relation to the question 'What areas of content are communicated?', or as we might put it, 'What is the teacher talking about?', the data are covered by Fanselow's categories *language* and *subject matter*. That is to say that the topics under discussion are either the language, as in Extract 2 below, or some information (including fictional information as in a story), or knowledge, as in Extract 3, or a mixture of the two, as in Extract 4:

### Extract 2

*T*: Let us use full sentences. Can you use a full sentence?

### Extract 3

*T*: Kyalo, is there a mountain near our school?

*Extract 4*

> *T*: How does a snake move? Eh?
>
> *P*: Walk.
>
> *T*: It walks? A snake walks? A snake does not walk. We say it 'crawls'.
>
> A snake crawls.

There are two content areas mentioned by Fanselow that are not represented in a significant way in the recordings. These are what Fanselow terms *life* and *procedure*.

The first, *life*, concerns communication about real life matters, such as the health of a child in the class or genuine discussion of feelings. The second, *procedure*, concerns those times when the teacher is managing the class, explaining what to do next, how to do it, and so on.[2] It is in these two areas that elicitations and responses are most likely to involve authentic communication, which some theorists (for example, Allwright, 1984a, 1984b; Ellis, 1984) have claimed can be particularly valuable for language acquisition in young children, since this is where the initiator is most likely to be asking 'real' questions (to which s/he does not know the answer) rather than pseudo-questions. As I explained above, it is the pseudo-question which is typical of the elicitations in the Kenyan data.

## ■ Teacher elicitation

In the data recorded by Oduol in the Kenyan primary classroom, five types of teacher elicitation can be identified. It can be seen that some examples take the form of questions, but other directives can also be observed.

*1 Questions*

> Did the police catch him? [A question about a thief in a story.]
>
> What type of houses do we find in the village? [A question to stimulate discussion for purposes of comparison.]

*2 Nominating*

> *T*: How can we move in the playground? Obunga.
>
> *P*: Jumping.
>
> *T*: 'Jumping'. We have heard of it. Berenda.
>
> *P*: Walking.

*3 Imperative*

> *T*: Everybody say 'pull'.
>
> *C*: Pull. Pull.

**4 Cue (in a structure drill; here to practise forming questions)**

*T*:  I am sitting down.

*C*:  Am I sitting down?

**5 Repetition as cue**

*T*:  Now ... ah ... Give me examples of liquid. Yes.

*P1*:  Water.

*T*:  Water, yes.

*P2*:  Ink, etc.

## ■ Learners' responses to elicitation

Data from native-speaker children (e.g. Sinclair and Coulthard, 1975) provide evidence that, in what we might call the 'normal' exchange, *elicitation* is followed by *response*. This is what Subbs calls a 'well-formed exchange'. He points out (p. 87) that, although we might think of human discourse as being something highly unpredictable, there are structures within that discourse which are predictable.

Hence, if a speaker fails to perform in the predicted way, in a particular situation, we feel that in some sense the discourse is ill-formed. This type of ill-formed discourse can occur in conversation with language-disordered children (see Stubbs, 1986, Ch. 10) and sometimes happens in native-speaker interaction, usually because a remark has been misheard. Stubbs gives the following example of an exchange between husband and wife, where *A* (the husband) immediately realises that the interaction is going wrong because of the ill-formed response of ***B*** (the wife):

*A*:  I'm going to do some weeding

*B*:  yes please

*A*:  what

*B*:  yes please

*A*:  you don't listen to anything I say

*B*:  I thought you said you were going to pour some drinks

*A*:  no I said I'm going to do some weeding

*B*'s response 'yes please' would only be appropriate in reply to an offer, and so the whole discourse is re-negotiated because the first *elicitation* was misheard.

However, in normal circumstances, ill-formedness in native-speaker interaction is rare even with quite young children. (See Phillips, 1985, for a discussion of the sophistication of the conversations of pre-school and first school native-speakers.)

In the African classroom recordings, however, there are innumerable examples of ill-formed exchanges, where the teacher's *elicitation* is followed by inappropriate responses at the level of interaction. The most striking form of ill-formedness is the non-response, where the pupil says nothing at all in response to a question. The non-response crops up again and again in the classroom recordings (and also, incidentally in the data of Reynolds, 1989). An example is given in Extract 5.

**Extract 5**

*T*:  Here is a picture of a village ... er ... a village. Look at the house.

[The picture shows some round houses with livestock in the background]

This is a village. [pointing]

Is Kangerni school in a town or is it in a village? Njoki?

*P*:  In a town.

*T*:  Yes ... Our school is in a town. It is not in a village. Now, who has been to a village? Who can tell us the things we can see in a village?

*P*:  [No response]

*T*:  A village ... A village ... What can we see in a village? Look at this picture. Tell me what you can see in this picture.

*P*:  [No response]

There are a number of different reasons that one could propose to explain learners' silence after an *elicitation*. Lack of space prevents detailed discussion here, but I list these, with brief explanatory notes, before going on to look at the ways in which teachers handle the problem:

1  *Socio-cultural reasons*. These include such factors as the reluctance of certain nationalities to talk in educational settings. Japanese and Finnish students are often cited by teachers who claim to have observed that they are reluctant to speak out in class because they have been trained to show respect by keeping silent.
2  *Personal psychological problems*. The student addressed is suffering from severe shyness, for example.
3  *Comprehension problems*. The student addressed doesn't understand what the teacher says.
4  *Expression problems*. The student understands and knows the correct response but can't express himself or herself in English.
5  *Knowledge problems*. The student doesn't know the answer.
6  *Pragmatic disorientation*. The student doesn't realise what the teacher is getting at. That is to say, he or she is not 'tuned in' to the teacher's wavelength, perhaps because of inattention.[3]

Without detailed discussion with learners in the mother-tongue by a researcher who is able to gain their confidence, it would be very difficult to establish the reasons why the children do not respond. That type of research (sometimes called protocol analysis) is rare and difficult to undertake. However, we can consider possible explanations and take them into account in our teaching.

In the case of the Kenyan classrooms, we can rule out the first two of the explanations in the above list because of the large number of different children involved and because of the number of well-formed exchanges. Since students often respond appropriately in these classrooms, we cannot propose socio-cultural or psychological problems as the cause of the instances of non-response. This leaves us with each of the final four explanations as possible contenders for each case.

One immediate practical outcome of looking at such data, is to re-emphasise the suggestion (made before by a number of people, including Willis, 1981) that all children should be taught very early in their course to express their reasons for non-response by asking for clarification, explaining lack of knowledge or their problems with expression. The teacher's task would be made easier if the children could voice such remarks as:

> I'm sorry. I don't understand.
>
> Would you please repeat that?
>
> What does ... mean?
>
> I'm afraid I don't know.
>
> I'm sorry. Let me try again.

The teaching of such expressions can 'give permission' to the children to behave honestly about non-comprehension, which can also help to free them from the tension of not knowing how to respond (see also Bloor, forthcoming).

It is not known how far native-speaker children use such expressions in the classroom. I suspect that often children prefer to give a wrong answer rather than admit to not knowing. Nevertheless very young native-speakers *can* use such language. Garvey (1975), for example, shows that children as young as three and a half will ask for clarification if they don't fully understand something that has been said to them, and Phillips (1985) gives other interesting examples of children's communicative skills.

## ■ Teachers as maintainers of communication

A useful activity for teachers in training is to consider how experienced teachers re-establish communication when the learner fails to respond to an elicitation. What do teachers do when a pupil fails to say anything in reply to a question? One thing is clear from the data: teachers have a number of different resources available to them.

Oduol showed that some teachers resort very quickly to using another language in order to re-establish communication. Such a change in the middle of a conversation from one language to another is known as 'code-switching'. In the Kenyan classes, teachers sometimes repeated the elicitation in Kiswahili (the other official language of education) if the students failed to respond to English. Such teachers made the assumption that the reason for non-response was lack of comprehension (the third reason in the list given above).

There are differences in the ways in which code-switching is used. Once communication is re-established, some teachers are content to stay with Kiswahili and may continue the lesson in that language, forgetting that English is supposed to be the language of instruction. Other teachers neatly reorientate the class into English medium, usually by reinitiating in English, as in Extract 6.

### Extract 6

> *T*: Now they are divided into two groups, and the groups are animals *with* a backbone and animals *without* a backbone. Where is the backbone?
>
> *P*: [No response]
>
> *T*: Backbone *ni huu mfupa uko hapa kwa mgongo.* It is this bone here at the back. Can you feel it is hard here?
>
> *P*: Yes.

This teacher uses the mother-tongue briefly to make a point but does not abandon English. She immediately repeats the information in English and then questions the children in English.

Some teachers never use Kiswahili, even though it is clear that they also feel that the learners have failed to understand the elicitation. In Extract 7 the teacher reformulates the first question 'Why can't they change?' by asking for the same information in a different way and the child gets the message and responds correctly.

### Extract 7

> [The teacher is discussing 'stones']
>
> *T*: Okay now. Why can't they change?
>
> *P*: [No response – eight seconds]
>
> *T*: They cannot grow bigger. They cannot grow smaller. Why?
>
> *P*: Because they are non-living.

Oduol called this a *modified elicitation*.

In other lessons, there is no attempt at rewording the question. The teacher completely replaces the first question with a different one (a *replacement elicitation*). In Extract 8 this happens after the teacher's first question gets no response:

### Extract 8

> *T*: What is ten divided by three?
>
> *P*: [No response]
>
> *T*: What is six divided by two?

It is likely that in this case the teacher attributes failure to respond to lack of knowledge rather than to non-comprehension. In Extract 9, it is difficult to decide on the exact reason for non-response to the question (about a story the class has heard), but we can see that the teacher again apparently uses a replacement elicitation:

### Extract 9

> *T*:  Now how did the crocodile and the monkey meet?
>
> *P*:  [No response]
>
> *T*:  The crocodile and the monkey? How did they meet?
>
> *P*:  [No response]
>
> *T*:  Does the monkey live in water?
>
> *P*:  No

However, further investigation reveals that the teacher has the next stage of the lesson in mind, including a way to help the children to answer the first question. The lesson continues:

### Extract 10

> *T*:  And the crocodile, does it live in water?
>
> *P*:  Yes.
>
> *T*:  So the monkey and the crocodile, how did they meet?
>
> *P*:  By the river.

The teacher is satisfied with this answer, and it seems likely that the wording of the teacher's first question ('How did they meet?') may have been unfortunate. Perhaps, if she had asked 'Where did they meet?', she would have received a readier response. In any case, the above dialogue illustrates clearly how the teacher (who was fairly experienced) resolved the problem, re-established communication and brought the pupil to a successful outcome.

Quite complex embedded exchanges can develop in teacher-directed lessons, some successful and some less successful. It is also clear from classroom data that teachers often use types of *preparatory elicitation*, that is, they use simpler elicitations to prepare the ground for more difficult ones. Such preparatory and embedded elicitations could prove a fruitful ground for observation, because if, as teachers, we can refine our use of such devices, we will be helped to plan lessons that develop the learners' comprehension of complex teaching materials.

Another interesting issue, which, as far as I know, has yet to be investigated, is whether or not teachers allow sufficient time for learners who are unfamiliar with English to formulate their responses. Certainly, the pauses are not long. If problems with expression are to blame for non-response (the fourth explanation offered in the list above), then pupils might respond if they were given more time.

# ■ Conclusion

In this discussion, I have tried to show how the analysis of classroom discourse can have interesting implications for teachers of non-native speakers of English who want to improve the ways in which communication takes place in their classrooms. The process involved interpreting messages that were communicated between other people in another country at another time. I don't for one moment think that I have always managed to get this right – although I do feel that I have learned something about my own communication with language learners in the process of trying.

The question of interpretation is an interesting one in itself. Candlin (1988) makes the point that 'the issue of description cannot be easily separated from interpretation ... and ... interpretation always implies a need for explanation.' This is important because without explanations for classroom problems we cannot begin to find ways of solving them.

If teachers and teachers in training can be given the opportunity to investigate such discoursal problems as communication breakdown and to propose explanations, awareness will develop and a variety of 'solutions' may be put to the test. Such awareness is of particular importance with classes of young learners because of the role played by interaction in all primary classrooms.

## Acknowledgement

Extracts from *Educational Linguistics*, Stubbs, are reproduced with the permission of Blackwell Publishers.

## Notes

1  A notable exception to this is the work of Reynolds (1988) and some of Allwright's own work.
2  Classroom management is, as a rule, conducted in English in classrooms in Kenya from Standard 4, but the limited nature of the activities, the shortage of resources, and the orderly behaviour of the children lead to minimal interaction on the subject.
3  My thanks to Rosalyn Hurst and Michael Burke for pointing out in discussion the sixth possible reason, which I have termed 'pragmatic disorientation'. I had overlooked this in an earlier draft.

# Part 5
# Teacher training and development

## Introduction

Throughout this Collection, reference has been made to the importance of the teacher in the implementation of plans to teach English language to young children. Part 5 looks at this aspect of primary level English language work more closely from three different perspectives.

Hayes' situation has much in common with the case studies described in Part 3, and his article demonstrates the linkage between syllabus design and teacher training. As described by Hayes, the Ministry of Education in Sabah implemented changes in the English language syllabus and methodology at primary level, moving from what had been a traditional approach to teaching and learning to one which put new demands on the teachers. These changes resulted in a large-scale programme of teacher training and development. Hayes shows how a 'cascade' model of training was used to implement the programme involving leaders, trainers and teachers.

What is interesting in this article is not only the content of the changes involved, but also the management of the various changes. Thus, at one level, it was important that trainers not only had knowledge of the new ELT content, but were also given training in the management of the means for delivering that content (the organisation of workshops, for example). At another level it is clear the programme organisers realised that changing teaching practices and methods is complex and sensitive and may, in certain circumstances, be seen as a threat. The article shows that mere explanation of change is not sufficient and that change imposed from above is unlikely to be longlasting. Hayes suggests a particular methodology which, by raising teachers' awareness and by encouraging teachers to question their practices, is more likely to lead to successful change.

Dickinson takes a narrower focus and looks at one particular aspect of teacher training programmes, that of the language competence of the teachers. If there is one factor that appears to be crucial in the successful implementation of primary level language programmes, it is the confidence of the teacher to use the language. The teachers that Dickinson trains put a high training priority on proficiency in English, placing language skills above purely pedagogic expertise. Low levels of language can lead to considerable teacher insecurity in the classroom which may prevent teachers going beyond language presented in the course book, something perhaps that native-speaker teacher trainers with their built-in linguistic advantage have tended to overlook.

Coleman reports on research conducted with teachers on class sizes and their relationship to methodology. The research throws up a number of facts that those working in more privileged settings would do well to ponder. The main interest however is not in the facts themselves, but in the use to which they can be put. Thus, information on teachers' attitudes to large classes and how they cope with the difficulties can provide valuable feedback to trainers so that the content of training courses can be made more relevant and appropriate to teachers in these situations. In addition, the sort of information Coleman describes can be collected by teachers themselves and used for self evaluation purposes. It is unlikely that teachers will have any influence over those who decide the size of their classes but, by collecting data similar to that described in Coleman's article and by exchanging such information with other teachers, they may be able to devise methodologies and techniques which can ease apparently intolerable situations.

# Primary ELT teachers and large classes

## Hywel Coleman

### ■ Introduction

This paper presents the findings of a questionnaire survey of primary ELT teachers working in the Sandakan division of Sabah in East Malaysia. The questionnaires used are reproduced in Appendices 1 and 2. They were developed by the Lancaster–Leeds Language Learning in Large Classes Research Project and have been used extensively elsewhere.

The questionnaires were given to a number of teachers involved in the Sabah Rural Primary English Programme (RuPEP) (see Hayes, this volume). Altogether, 38 responses were received, of which 17 were anonymous. Of the 38 teachers who responded to the questionnaire, five (13 per cent) believe that large classes constitute their major problem, 29 (76 per cent) say that large classes are one of the major problems facing them, and three (8 per cent) perceive large classes to be a problem, but not a major one. One teacher (i.e. 3 per cent of the population) did not indicate how severe he/she perceived the problem to be.

### ■ Class size

The numbers of pupils in the classes taught by the group of teachers who participated in this survey are summarised in Table 1. The teachers work with classes which range in size from five to 60. The average size of the *largest* class which they normally teach is 47.2, though the largest classes range from 32 to 60. The average size of the *usual* class is 43.5 (ranging from 30 to 55). And the average size of the *smallest* class is 39.3 (ranging from five to 50). Thus, the smallest class experienced by some of these respondents (50) is larger than the largest experienced by other respondents (32).

| Table 1 | Class sizes experienced by teachers | | |
|---|---|---|---|
| | Average | Range | Respondents (N) |
| largest | 47.2 | 32-60 | 38 |
| usual | 43.5 | 30-55 | 30 |
| smallest | 39.3 | 5-50 | 37 |

Whilst Table 1 presents the class sizes which teachers actually experience, Table 2 summarises the *perceptions* of the same teachers regarding class size. For these teachers, the ideal class may have from 15 to 40 pupils (average 27.7). When numbers reach 39.6, problems begin because the class is getting too large, and when they reach 47.5 the class is considered to be intolerably large. For some teachers, however, the situation becomes intolerable only when numbers reach 65.

| Table 2 | Teachers' perceptions of class sizes | | |
|---|---|---|---|
| | **Average** | **Range** | **Respondents (N)** |
| intolerably large | 47.5 | 32-65 | 29 |
| problems begin because large | 39.6 | 20-60 | 38 |
| ideal | 27.7 | 15-40 | 38 |
| problems begin because small | 12.0 | 3-30 | 18 |
| intolerably small | 6.3 | 2-25 | 14 |

Teachers also believe that a class may be *too small*. For these teachers, problems begin when numbers drop to 12.0, and the class is intolerably small when it has 6.3 pupils, although for some teachers even a class of 25 may be considered to be intolerably small. What is particularly interesting to note here is that fewer than half of the respondents answered the questions about small classes. The reason which teachers usually give for not answering these two questions is simply that they have no experience of teaching classes which they consider to be too small. Even those who do answer these questions often say that they are guessing, because teaching small classes is something which lies outside their experience. It was not possible to check with this particular group of teachers in Sabah, but we can assume that – like their colleagues elsewhere – very few of them have taught classes which they consider to be small.

Now, if we superimpose Table 1 upon Table 2, we produce Table 3, which allows us to compare the experience and the perception of the teachers. Some very interesting things emerge. Firstly, we find that, as a group, the largest classes which the teachers normally work with (47.2) have reached almost precisely the point (47.5) where the situation is intolerable. In fact, many of these individual respondents are teaching classes which are already larger than the points which they consider intolerable. The second matter of interest is that the average size of the usual classes which the teachers teach (43.5) is itself larger than the point at which they begin to experience problems (39.6). In other words, the average primary ELT teacher among this group experiences problems because of class size even in ordinary situations. The third point to observe is that the smallest classes which these teachers experience (39.3) are themselves barely below the point at which problems start (39.6); that is to say, even the smallest classes are at or around the size where teaching becomes difficult because classes are so large. Not surprisingly, the ideal class size which these teachers would like to work with (27.7) is considerably smaller than even their smallest classes (39.3).

| Table 3 | Experience and perception compared | |
|---|---|---|
| **Experience** | | **Perception** |
| | 47.5 | intolerably large |
| largest | 47.2 | |
| usual | 43.5 | |
| | 39.6 | problems begin because large |
| smallest | 39.3 | |
| | 27.7 | ideal |
| | 12.0 | problems begin because small |
| | 6.3 | intolerably small |

From the figures in Tables 1–3, we can conclude that this group of teachers is working in a situation which, by their own definition, is difficult and in some cases intolerable.

## ■ Techniques for large classes

Given that the teachers are working in such difficult conditions, what techniques do they employ to help their learners learn in large classes? Of the 38 respondents, 29 (76 per cent) answered this question, mentioning a total of 74 techniques (2.6 techniques per person responding to the question). Some techniques were mentioned by several different teachers, and so it is possible to classify them fairly easily into ten categories. These are shown in Table 4. The two most frequently mentioned techniques are the use of groups and pairs, and the use of visual aids. The next most frequently employed techniques are drills and songs. We can illustrate these categories with extracts from the teachers' own responses.[1]

| Table 4 | Techniques currently used by teachers in large classes | |
| --- | --- | --- |
| Categories of technique | Respondents (N = 29) | Number of techniques reported |
| 1   Using groups and pairs | 14 | 17 |
| 2   Visual aids, etc. | 13 | 14 |
| 3   Drills | 6 | 7 |
| 4   Songs | 6 | 6 |
| 5   Oral work | 3 | 4 |
| 6   Helping weaker learners | 3 | 3 |
| 7   Demonstrations | 3 | 3 |
| 8   Translation | 2 | 2 |
| 9   Games | 2 | 2 |
| 10   Miscellaneous techniques | 12 | 16 |
| **Total** | 29 | 74 |

## Using groups and pairs

Fourteen teachers listed a total of 17 techniques which can be classified under the heading of 'groups and pairs'. Some teachers observe that they divide groups according to proficiency:

Dividing into groups of various levels. (Teacher 13)

Dividing the class into several groups, such as good, moderate and poor. (Teacher 15)

Other teachers, however, prefer to use mixed ability groups:

Dividing the pupils in groups to give more group activities. Mix the above groups with good/weak students which will help the weaker ones. (Teacher 14)

Some teachers are concerned with the selection and responsibilities of group leaders:

Group teaching; each group select a group leader who is good in English and helpful. (Teacher 35)

### Visual aids

Thirteen teachers report using a total of 14 techniques which fall under this heading. The majority simply observe that they make use of pictures or other aids:

> Showing colourful pictures. (Teacher 27)
>
> Using visual materials and etc. to make the lesson more interesting, and make them can understand the lesson easily. (Teacher 36)

One teacher, however, comments that when using visual aids he/she tries to imagine that the whole class is of a uniform standard, despite the fact that large classes inevitably involve considerable heterogeneity:

> Using visual aids and keeping in my mind that I am teaching student in the average standard (even though these are students in different standard). (Teacher 12)

### Miscellaneous techniques

The 'miscellaneous' category covers a wide range of classroom management procedures. One teacher feels that in a large class it is possible to do little more than police the learners and correct their mistakes:

> Just going around the class, only paying attention to few students each period. Time isn't suitable, so generally I correct their mistakes in class. (Teacher 2)

Another feels that the most suitable way of managing large classes is to motivate the pupils by arousing competition between them:

> Creative competative achievement programme so that pupils will compete to get better results. (Teacher 14)

### Summary

It is encouraging, but also rather surprising, that so many of these teachers claim that they are already using groups as a way of overcoming the problems created by large class size.

These responses are surprising for two reasons. Firstly, as we shall see in later parts of this discussion, the same teachers claim that they have difficulty in using groups in large classes. They also feel that, if they had smaller numbers, then they would find it easier to use groups in their teaching. In other words, some of them seem to have adopted a technique which they actually find difficult. The second reason for finding this claim to use groups surprising is that very many teachers of large classes in different parts of the world appear to be reluctant to contemplate the possibility of using groups in their teaching. Their perception is that groupwork is precisely the sort of activity which is impossible in large classes.

It is therefore encouraging to know that, at least among the Sabah teachers surveyed here, nearly half employ groupwork as their primary measure for managing large classes, *even if* they still experience some difficulties in doing so.

# ■ Difficulties in large classes

Let us now move on to look in detail at the difficulties which the teachers experience when teaching large classes. All 38 teachers involved in the survey responded to this question and, between them, they reported a total of 124 difficulties (3.3 difficulties per person).

| Table 5 | Difficulties experienced by teachers in large classes | | |
|---|---|---|---|
| Catergories of difficulty | Respondents (N = 38) | Number of difficulties reported | |
| 1 Classroom management | 35 | | 61 |
| 1.1 Control and discipline | 28 | 33 | |
| 1.2 Noise | 8 | 8 | |
| 1.3 Overcrowding and restricted movement | 8 | 8 | |
| 1.4 Forming and using groups | 7 | 7 | |
| 1.5 Management of activities | 5 | 5 | |
| 2 Paying attention to learners | 28 | | 39 |
| 2.1 Paying attention to individuals | 18 | 20 | |
| 2.2 Helping weaker learners | 11 | 13 | |
| 2.3 Involving all learners | 4 | 4 | |
| 2.4 Helping stronger learners | 2 | 2 | |
| 3 Preparation of materials | 12 | | 13 |
| 4 Time | 6 | | 6 |
| 5 Providing feedback | 6 | | 6 |
| 6 Miscellaneous difficulties | 6 | | 7 |
| Total | 38 | | 124 |

There are five major categories of difficulty, shown in Table 5 (classroom management, paying attention to learners, preparation of materials, time, and providing feedback). Two of the major categories are subdivided. Almost half of all the reported difficulties fall into the major category of 'classroom management' (61 out of 124: 49.2 per cent). A further 31.5 per cent of responses (39 out of 124) come under the heading of 'paying attention to learners'.

At first sight, this may give the impression that teachers' concern with the maintenance of control far outweighs their concern for the well-being of their learners. However, if we treat the subcategories in Table 5 as categories in their own right, and rearrange them in order of the frequency with which they are mentioned, we find that the four most important types of difficulty are as follows:

1.1    Control and discipline        (33)
2.1    Paying attention to individuals    (20)
2.2    Helping weaker learners        (13)
3      Preparation of materials        (13)

Difficulties of control and discipline still predominate. But these teachers are also very worried by the difficulty which they experience in their large classes in trying to pay individual attention to learners, helping weaker learners, and preparing materials. That is to say, even though these teachers are working in very difficult conditions – often, as we have already seen, in situations which are intolerable – they still feel that they *ought* to be paying attention to individuals, helping the weaker ones, and preparing materials.

We can select the most important categories and subcategories of difficulty and look at some of the teachers' responses.

### Classroom management

Thirty-five teachers complain of difficulties in this area, with 61 individual problems reported.

### Control and discipline

As we have seen, this is by far the most numerous category of difficulties which teachers experience: 28 of the 38 respondents report problems here. Interestingly, 27 of these teachers use the word 'control' in their comments.

### Noise

Eight respondents perceive noise to be a problem:

> I have to volume my voice every time I begin a lesson. (It hurts my throat.) (Teacher 7)
>
> It gets too noisy when I'm doing a one to one question and answer with the pupils. (Teacher 27)

### Overcrowding and restricted movement

This is a problem reported by eight teachers:

> No ways for the teacher to get around because of the class size is uncomfortable. (Teacher 24)

### Forming and using groups

We have already noticed that a majority of the teachers who participated in this survey claim that they use groupwork as a procedure for overcoming the problem of large classes, and that this is rather unusual compared to large class teachers in other parts of the world. Nevertheless, seven of the respondents complain that using groups in large classes is difficult or impossible:

> As the class consist more than 50 pupils, it is quite hard to carry out group activities because pupils tends to talk and play more than carrying out the activities assigned to them. As result of it, teacher seldom carry out group activities. (Teacher 11)

## Paying attention to learners

Altogether 39 comments were made by 28 teachers in this category. We will look at extracts which illustrate just two of the four subcategories.

### Paying attention to individuals

Eighteen teachers say that they have difficulty in this area; 20 different problems were reported:

> Impossible to see into individual pupil's problem for every lesson. (Teacher 2)

> And also I can't teach each one of the student in the large classes, may be some of them can't understand the lesson. (Teacher 36)

### Helping weaker learners

Eleven teachers experience difficulty in helping weaker learners in their large classes; 13 different comments were made here. It is significant that some of the longest and most detailed comments were made in this area:

> There are too many slow students in a class that some of them are left out while teaching. I couldn't give my undivided attention to them ... The education here is exam oriented so I have to cover the syllabus. If I go fast the good children get it and the poor ones are left out. (Teacher 8)

> When a class consist of more than 50 pupils, nearly 2/3 of the pupils are weak and to this, teacher can't pay more attention to the weak ones ... As our government is exam orientated, so most of the teachers tend to cover the syllabus as fast as possible just in order to finish it but they never take into account that their pupils might not have mastered the skills or certain skills, especially the weak ones. (Teacher 11)

> To many students in a group, so couldn't detect boys who cannot read or write. (Teacher 20)

> If the students are not good from their basics (reading and writing) its too difficult for the teacher to help them individually during teaching lesson. (Teacher 25)

### Preparation of materials

Preparing enough materials for all the pupils in large classes is a difficulty mentioned by twelve teachers. Their comments are generally brief, such as the following:

> Not enough teaching materials provided and teachers can't make a lot of them if the size of the class is too big, specially in group activities. (Teacher 11)

### Providing feedback

The problem of marking the written work of learners is one of the difficulties which is most frequently mentioned by teachers of large classes throughout the world. Rather surprisingly, only six of the 38 teachers participating in this survey mention marking as a problem:

> Too many exercise books to be corrected and to call individual pupils to point out their mistakes and solve the problems they are facing in the third language. [in Chinese Medium School] (Teacher 2)

> Giving too many work for consolidating in certain items make me tired of marking and commenting on the papers. (Teacher 14)

Many teachers, then, both in Sabah and elsewhere, complain about the burden of providing feedback on children's written work. It is important to note that this providing of feedback tends largely to be a process of identifying and correcting errors. When we observe teachers working in large classes, we very frequently find that much of their time and effort is expended in a parallel process of identifying and correcting oral errors. In other words, the workload of many teachers of large classes is dominated by two closely related types of activity: correcting written errors and correcting spoken errors. Teachers apparently recognise the correcting of written errors as a problem associated with the teaching of large classes, yet very few of them report the correction of oral errors to be a problem in the same way. It may be that the correcting of oral errors in the classroom is seen to be central to the role of a teacher, whilst the correcting of written work – probably carried out outside teaching hours – is perhaps perceived as somehow more peripheral.

### ■ In an ideal class ...

We have been looking in detail at the difficulties which teachers report. The questionnaire (Appendix 2) also asked teachers to complete the statement: 'With an ideal number of students in my class, I could ...' Thirty-four of the teachers responded to this question and provided 98 expected outcomes which they believe would occur if they could teach in an ideal class (2.9 comments per teacher).

These responses can be categorised, again using an *ad hoc* system. The result is shown in Table 6. The two most significant groups of outcome come under the headings 'Classroom management' and 'Paying attention to learners', whilst the four most frequently mentioned categories of outcome are as follows:

1.1      Control and discipline          (22)
2.1      Paying attention to individuals  (12)
2.2      Helping weaker learners          (12)
1.2      Forming and using groups          (9)

It can be seen immediately that Table 6 is very similar to Table 5. This indicates that, not surprisingly, the outcomes which teachers would expect from an ideal size class are the mirror images of the difficulties which they currently encounter in teaching large classes.

| Table 6  Outcomes expected by teachers from an ideal size class | | |
|---|---|---|
| Categories of outcome | Respondents (N = 38) | Number of outcomes expected |
| 1  Classroom management | 24 | 44 |
| 1.1  Control and discipline | 20 | 22 |
| 1.2  Forming and using groups | 8 | 9 |
| 1.3  Management of activities | 6 | 7 |
| 1.4  Noise | 3 | 3 |
| 1.5  Overcrowding and restricted movement | 2 | 3 |
| 2  Paying attention to learners | 25 | 26 |
| 2.1  Paying attention to individuals | 12 | 12 |
| 2.2  Helping weaker learners | 12 | 12 |
| 2.3  Involving all learners | 2 | 2 |
| 3  Preparation of materials | 6 | 6 |
| 4  Providing feedback | 5 | 6 |
| 5  Miscellaneous techniques | 6 | 7 |
| 6  General improvement | 9 | 9 |
| Total | 34 | 98 |

## ■ Conclusions

We have seen that this group of 38 primary teachers of ELT, who are working in one administrative division of Sabah in East Malaysia, find themselves in a situation where they face classes with an average size of 43.5, but ranging up to 60. By their own definition, many of these teachers are therefore teaching in conditions which are very nearly intolerable or indeed are already intolerable. In attempting to deal with this situation, they use a variety of techniques and procedures, amongst which the use of groups and of visual aids are the most important. For these teachers, trying to teach in large classes poses many problems, including classroom control, paying attention to individuals, helping weaker learners, and preparing materials for large numbers of learners. If class sizes could be reduced to a point which they consider to be ideal (27.7 for the average teacher), then the teachers believe that teaching would become easier for them in several different ways, but especially in control and discipline of the class, in paying attention to individuals, in helping weaker learners, and in using groups.

At various points during this discussion, we have pointed out similarities and contrasts with the attitudes of large class teachers in other parts of the world. The similarities predominate. Teachers of large classes in most situations appear to be concerned about control, evaluation, getting to know their learners as individuals, and whether or not their learners are actually learning anything (Coleman, 1989c). The differences lie only in the relative significance which teachers attach to the various difficulties. As we have seen, the question of control was the most frequently mentioned problem for the teachers in Sabah. On the other hand, Peachey (1989), looking at the attitudes of black primary school teachers in South Africa, found that, for this group, paying attention to individuals and preparing teaching materials were overwhelmingly the most frequently listed problems which they had to face. Discipline or control was also perceived as a problem by the South African teachers, but it ranked only as approximately the tenth most important difficulty. Meanwhile, Coleman (1989b), in his study of the attitudes of Nigerian university teachers of large classes, discovered that paying attention to individual learners ranked as the most commonly mentioned problem (as with the South African teachers). This was followed by control and then by evaluation.

Where do we go from here? The value of studies such as this probably lies in three areas. Firstly, this analysis raises questions for those who are concerned with primary ELT in the specific context of Sabah. Why, for example, is classroom control considered by these teachers to be of such significance? In other words, an investigation such as this one may contribute a little to the understanding which administrators, teacher educators and teachers themselves have of their own situation.

Secondly, on a much wider scale, an analysis such as this one contributes to our growing knowledge of large classes in general. The more such studies become available, the easier it will become for us to determine what is unique about large classes in a particular situation and what universal features large classes share.

Finally, and most importantly, an understanding of the way in which teachers perceive their own large classes may provide the foundation for practical action to bring about change in the management of large classes. Coleman (1989c) has suggested that teachers should be encouraged to analyse their self-reported difficulties in working with large classes. Then, on the basis of these analyses, teachers can formulate principles against which they can evaluate proposals for change. It is hoped that this discussion of the attitudes of large class teachers in Sabah may contribute to this effort.

## Acknowledgement

I am grateful to George Taylor for administering the questionnaires on which this discussion is based. I am also grateful to David Hayes, who provided background information about the teachers whose responses are studied here, and to Trevor Grimshaw, who commented on an earlier version of this paper.

## Notes

1  All the extracts from the teachers' questionnaire responses are reproduced precisely as they were written.

**Appendix 1**
Important: please think only of *English Language* classes.

1  How many people are there:
   (a) in the largest class which you regularly teach?
   (b) in the smallest class which you regularly teach?

2  What is your usual class size?

3  What is your ideal class size?

4  What class size do you consider to be uncomfortably large?
   (a) At what number do the problems begin?
   (b) At what number do the problems become intolerable?

5  What class size do you consider to be uncomfortably small?
   (a) At what number do the problems begin?
   (b) At what number do the problems become intolerable?

6  Among all your problems, how important is class size? Is dealing with large classes (please ring the appropriate letter):
   the major problem                               a
   one of the major problems                       b
   a problem, but not a major one                  c
   a very minor problem                            d
   no problem at all                               e

7  Is the institution you teach in (please ring the appropriate letter):
   primary/elementary?                             a
   secondary?                                      b
   college/university?                             c
   other (please specify)?                         d
*(Lancaster–Leeds Language Learning in Large Classes Research Project)*

**Appendix 2**

Many teachers say that teaching English in large classes is a problem for them. But in what way are large classes a problem? How do large classes stop teachers from doing what they would like to do? Your responses to this questionnaire will help us to answer these questions.

Under each of the following, please list as many points as you can.

1 *Large classes* make it difficult for me to do what I would like to do because:

2 With an *ideal* number of students in my class, I could:

3 When I am teaching a *large class*, I help my students to learn English by:

4 Do you have any other comments or questions about teaching and learning in *large classes*?

5 Is the institution you teach in (please ring the appropriate letter):
primary/elementary?                                                             a
secondary?                                                                      b
college/university?                                                             c
other (please specify)?                                                         d

6 In principle, would you be willing to help us with future research into large classes (perhaps by responding to another questionnaire)? **Yes/No**

Thank you very much for your help.
*(Lancaster–Leeds Language Learning in Large Classes Research Project)*

# Classroom language – what do primary school ELT teachers need to know?

## Norma Dickinson

How best to train teachers from developing countries is a question constantly under discussion. Those teachers who are sent to the UK for training are non-typical in that they are well above the average level of teachers in their home country in proficiency in English, in professional attitudes, self-confidence and motivation. When they go back home they will almost certainly be involved in innovation in classroom methodology at some level, so preparation for this is necessary.

In the Moray House Edinburgh programme one of the topics regularly looked at every year is that of classroom language in relation to teachers' proficiency in English; one aspect of this is the desirability of getting teachers in an EFL situation to conduct the ordinary management of the class in English and to encourage the learners to respond to the teacher in English in classroom activities. This has been well discussed and documented in Willis (1981) for the post-primary level and Dunn (1985) for the primary level. The relevant classroom language has been listed in Hughes, 1981. Clark's description of the work done in the GLAFLL project describes the same process for a foreign language in a UK setting (Clark, 1987). Helping pupils to use English in classroom management tasks is just one aspect of the attempt to make English (or any other target language) a language of meaningful communication in the classroom.

In our seminars the first topic normally considered is what item of language the learners could learn to use in the classroom to carry out day-to-day management tasks, and we spend some time discussing how closely these items of language have to relate to the syllabus or textbook. Many teachers find the notion of teaching 'beyond' or 'outside' the current linguistic level of the learner too disturbing an idea to accept, let alone describe to other teachers back home. Sometimes an item is taken from the syllabus and we try to relate this item to language that is appropriate for classroom management tasks. However, it is not the identification of useful language or the relating (or non-relating) of these language items to the syllabus that cause difficulties in implementation. The real difficulty is the level of English of the primary school teacher (who is not usually a specialist English teacher) and the resulting lack of confidence and low self-esteem which leads to overwhelming reluctance to innovate or even to 'go beyond' the words that are printed on the page of the textbook.

I thought it might be revealing to ask a group of primary level practitioners from Europe who had differing experiences in ES/FL in a variety of countries how they would react to the problem of primary school EFL teachers with low competence in English, so that their reactions could be compared to the reactions of teachers from developing countries. The situations that we discuss in class are set in developing countries.

The question that starts off my seminar/discussions with my overseas teachers is:

What kind of teachers would be confident enough

1 to teach their pupils the appropriate language for classroom organisation tasks and

2 to encourage them to use that language?

This question can be analysed into three other questions:

1 What level of language knowledge/proficiency would such a teacher need to have?

2 What type of pedagogic skills would such a teacher need to have?

3 What sort of attitudes to learner participation would such a teacher need to have?

Finally, we consider the question – which of these three aspects would you (as a supervisor/trainer) select to concentrate on first?

It is possible to sketch out what would be a desirable (but perhaps not a very realistic) profile of primary school teachers in a developing country. They would have studied English throughout their secondary school career, which should have been at least four years. In certain contexts they would have studied English at primary level as well, though many overseas teachers debate the usefulness of studying English at primary level because of the lack of resources to do so adequately. The literature on age differences in language learning seems to indicate that children under ten put in a situation where they can *acquire* a language, i.e. they are in a country where the target language is spoken, are more successful than adults, particularly with regard to the phonological system (Dulay et al., 1982). The assumption being made is, of course, that they are being taught by native-speakers as well as meeting them outside school. There is little available research on young children being taught by non-native speakers of English who lack confidence in their ability to speak and learn English in surroundings where English is never spoken outside the classroom. To repeat – the ideal teacher should have studied English at secondary level for at least four years and the school examination system should have had an oral component.

Secondly, the primary school teacher should have had training for primary school teaching: in developing countries this is normally two years. In this course there should have been, at least, a component on how children learn to speak the mother-tongue and to read and write, i.e. a basic component on first and second language acquisition and learning. Also there should have been a component on how to teach a foreign/second language with particular reference to how to teach a new script (if this is relevant).

Lastly, the trainee teacher should have been made aware of the relationship between teaching and learning and between input and output, since the input received by children in most countries where English is taught at primary school level derives totally from the teachers.

Of course, there are many other components that ought to be in such a teacher training course (not least an English improvement course for the trainee teachers) but it is unrealistic to expect too much from a two-year course for a generalist teacher at primary school level. In reality, primary school teachers are often like those described on the three situation sheets (see Appendix 1).

Are the three components listed all equally significant for a teacher? Normally my seminar discussions on this topic end with all the course members firmly ranged against me. I argue that these three aspects are all equally important: the teachers argue that proficiency in English is far more significant that the others; they argue that pedagogic skills and appropriate attitudes to learner participation arise from the confidence that derives from an adequate command of the language. They contend that inability to 'function adequately' in English is a state a native-speaker of English has never experienced and therefore the native-speaker knows nothing of the inhibitory effects such inadequacy has on pedagogic development, receptiveness to new ideas and the whole affective domain. Therefore they would use any in-service training time on language improvement.

As I said earlier, it seemed it would be interesting to ask the Leeds seminar participants for their reactions. They were presented with three of the scenarios used in the Moray House workshops.

The results of the discussion at the Leeds seminar were inconclusive because there was insufficient time to discuss the topics thoroughly. The composition of the groups discussing the three scenarios was not sufficiently identified for comparison with the overseas teachers' groups. They were almost all either native-speakers of English, most of whom had experience working overseas in developing countries, or teachers from other European Community countries. In addition, the Leeds participants even when working in developing countries had been working in a 'British' framework and not in a 'developing country' framework (unless they had been VSOs).[1] Also at Leeds the question of whether or not it was really realistic to ask teachers to use and help learners to use English for a few classroom management activities was not highlighted (lack of time) but one group did discuss it.

The outcome of the discussions was that of the three groups discussing the scenarios only one took the teacher's language proficiency as being something they would attempt to improve in two days of in-service work. A second group decided that teachers such as those described in the scenarios would not be prepared to use any English they did not find on the printed pages of their textbooks and would certainly not teach their pupils to use English for classroom management tasks. They saw these demands as being quite unrealistic. The third group, where the scenario offered the availability of a radio programme in English, decided that they would probably spend half of the seminar introducing their participants to tape-recordings of the radio broadcast, training them to listen and then using the materials for oral interaction. By keying these teachers into the broadcasts it was hoped that they would continue to listen to them; this would, to some extent, raise their professional awareness as well as improve their listening skills.

Where the Leeds participants agreed with the teachers from developing countries is in the importance of the affective domain. They listed:

1 The need to make teachers participating in the seminars feel 'special'. The Leeds participants suggested using some of the money:
   (a) for a party/lunch;
   (b) to establish a small local newsletter, for the participants initially, but involving other teachers as soon as possible. The newsletter was intended to:
      (i) foster the attitudes to reflecting about one's teaching, identifying the areas of difficulty, the solutions to which might be shared;

  (ii) establish feelings of community in relation to the difficulties found in teaching English as a foreign language.

2 Another suggested way of making the workshop memorable was to spend two days (whether separate or together) doing drama. Drama in small groups was seen as providing:

  (a) the opportunity to emphasise co-operative rather than individual work;

  (b) an opportunity for participants to *use* the English they have and to become aware of the need for more English to express themselves;

  (c) an opportunity for the supervisor of the seminar to provide correct versions of grammatically deviant structures *without* appearing to be correcting language;

  (d) an awareness of how dramatic activities might be useful in their classroom.

This awareness-raising would be the last section of the workshop. However, the main reason for using drama was that it would provide an enjoyable experience.

The emphasis on making the experience enjoyable is one which supervisors from developing countries also see as being important. They see a meal/party as being a motivating part of a workshop, as well as giving a notebook to keep as an ordinary/educational diary. Designating attenders at INSET workshops as key teachers was also seen as being motivating.

Teachers from developing countries seem to be less aware (though possibly this is caused by a failure to be explicit) about the importance of working from what teachers already know/have. Of course it may also be that they are in a position to feel more free to express dissatisfaction with their fellow teachers and to emphasise the necessity for teachers to improve their own language proficiency. Such improvement is seen as an essential first step to heighten awareness of the need for improved pedagogic skills in general and the need for using the target language in classroom language in particular. Therefore they argue strongly that in-service time should be spent on language improvement, especially on grammatical improvement. We as native-speaker teacher trainers are understandably reluctant to point out the deficiencies in the level of English of primary school teachers in developing countries. We do not see this as our business – and maybe it is not. However, our emphasis on improving pedagogic skills and raising awareness of the affective domain is often seen as 'beating in the dark' because we have refused to look at the teacher's underlying lack of confidence which is a result of their self-knowledge about their low level of English proficiency.

## Note

1 VSO (Voluntary Service Overseas) is an organisation which recruits volunteer teachers from the UK to work in the developing world.

Appendix 1

# SITUATION 1

Country - in West Africa.

## Language

There are several local languages. English is a lingua franca and is the medium of instruction in all schools. People speak a creole outside the classroom and pupils sometimes use it in the classroom to communicate but more often they use their local language which differs from area to area.

## Classroom language

According to the Ministry of Education, English should be used in the classroom for all interaction between teacher and pupils. In reality, many teachers use the local language to talk to pupils and to teach in because of their lack of confidence in using English.

## Typical Teachers.

Seventy five per cent of primary school teachers are untrained. Because they have failed some subjects in their School Certificate they cannot get into college or into the Civil Service but they can get accepted as primary school teachers. Most of them want to resit their Certificate so they do not see their careers in primary schools. However, if they teach in primary schools for three years and then get a good report they may be eligible for a teacher training course in a college (but there are not sufficient places for all those who are eligible).

## Classroom Behaviour

Teachers are required to:
(a)   teach English so that their pupils' proficiency improves.
(b)   to use English to teach English.
(c)   to teach other subjects in the medium of English.

All primary school pupils have been taught to read in English but many pupils at every level have still not mastered reading although they can recognise occasional words. Teachers teach English by very traditional ways - as they themselves were taught. They read out sentences and the pupils repeat. They write on the blackboard and the pupils copy. Pupils never use English in a meaningful way. Books which are reasonably modern and up-to-date are provided but usually there are insufficient copies for the large classes.

## Size of Classes

50 - 70

Imagine you are asked to indicate what recommendations you would make about helping these young, unmotivated, untrained teachers to train pupils to use English for ordinary everyday classroom management tasks in these scenarios.

## Scenario 1.

You have two days of inservice input per year and a very small sum of money.

## Scenario 2.

You have one week of inservice per year and rather more money than in one above but still a realistic amount for a developing country.

Image you are the local VSO. You have got 34 teachers of primary 4 (ages 9-12) in your area. You have decided to work with the teachers at this level. Would you concentrate on:
(1)   improving their language knowledge.
(2)   raising Awareness of the relevant pedagogic skills.
(3)   altering attitudes to learner participation.
(4)   all of these?

INDICATE AS PRECISELY AS POSSIBLE WHAT YOU WOULD DO TO HELP THESE TEACHERS USING FIRST SCENARIO 1 AND SECONDLY SCENARIO 2. YOU SHOULD MAKE AT LEAST **THREE** RECOMMENDATIONS FOR EACH SCENARIO.

# SITUATION 2

**Country** - in East Africa.

**Language**.
The national language is used everywhere outside school and in school - it is the medium of instruction. There are some local languages but everyone in school has to learn the national language.

**Classroom Language**.
The national language is the medium of instruction for all subjects except English. English is taught as a subject at the primary level. The script of English is the same as the script of the national language but nevertheless learning to read in English is a difficult task for most learners.

The teaching of English cannot be neglected because:
(a) a good pass in English is necessary for admission to secondary education where places are limited. In all secondary schools the medium of instruction is English so it is important that pupils going up from primary school have a basic knowledge of English.
(b) if pupils pass well in all other subjects in the secondary exam and do poorly in English the local primary school inspector is supposed to go to the teacher to discuss why this has happened.

**Typical Teachers**.
Many of the teachers have had a two year primary school teacher training. Other teachers went into teaching without any training but they are supposed to get trained by weekly inservice inputs and this is feasible if they live in the towns. The official teacher training course would include the teaching of English as a subject. The teacher him/herself would have studied in English for at least two years in secondary school and perhaps for as many as four years.

The teacher that you are going to deal with has had four years of English in secondary school and then a two year teacher training course which trained the teacher to cover all the subjects in the primary school, including English.

**Classroom Behaviour**.
There are books provided which are based upon the syllabus drawn up in 1982-84. These books are fairly traditional and they emphasise the reading skill though some oral and written work is supposed to be done. Reading is emphasised because:
(1) many teachers are not very competent teaching oral English.
(2) reading English is very important in the secondary education sector where all the text books are in English.

**Class Size**.
This varies from 50 - 80. A class of 60 in the country areas is likely to be a composite class at 2 or 3 levels. Imagine you are asked to indicate what recommendations you would make about helping a middle-aged trained (20 years ago) teacher in the country whose class is 60 pupils at 3 levels to train pupils to use English for ordinary everyday classroom management tasks in these scenarios.

**Scenario 1**.
You have 2 days of inservice input per year and a very small sum of money.

**Scenario 2**
You have one week of inservice per year and rather more money than in one above but still a realistic amount for a developing country.

Imagine you are the local VSO. You have got 34 teachers of primary 4 (ages 9-12) in your area. You have decided to work with the teachers at this level. Would you concentrate on:
(1) improving their language knowledge.
(2) raising awareness of the relevant pedagogic skills.
(3) altering attitudes to learner participation
(4) all of these?

INDICATE AS PRECISELY AS POSSIBLE WHAT YOU WOULD DO TO HELP THESE TEACHERS USING FIRST SCENARIO 1 AND SECONDLY SCENARIO 2. YOU SHOULD MAKE AT LEAST **THREE** RECOMMENDATIONS FOR EACH SCENARIO.

# SITUATION 3

**Country** - a State in India.

**Language**.
The language of everyday communication of newspapers, of the provincial government etc. is Gujarati (recognised by the Indian Government as one of the main Indian languages).

**Classroom Language**.
The language of the classroom and the medium for instruction at all levels in the schools system is Gujarati. Formerly English was a subject at the secondary level. Because of political pressures for English in the primary school this was "inflicted from above' in 1977 without any consultation, preparation or funding. However, a choice was given to the Districts within the state; District School Boards were allowed to choose whether or not they would teach English at the primary level. Currently some two-thirds of the school districts in the state have opted to teach English at the primary level. The other remaining third is supposed to do so at some future unspecified date.

Pupils start to learn English as a subject in class 6 of the primary school when they are aged 8-10 years old and they learn it in class 7 and 8 as well. Then they finish primary school. English is taught by the primary school class teacher as well as all the other primary school subjects. At all times English is taught through the medium of Gujarati. Secondary school starts in class 9 and English is once again taught as a subject. Because not all of the pupils going into secondary school have studied English in the primary school it is necessary to start teaching English again from the very beginning i.e. the teaching of the script of English in the first class in the secondary school. It is clear that many teachers do not really bother very hard to teach English in the primary school because they know that their pupils will get a chance to learn it in the secondary school.

**Typical Teachers**.
Primary school teachers tend to leave secondary school after two years when they are aged about 16-18. They have all studied English for these two years in secondary school but it is not a compulsory examination subject so they may never have sat an examination in English. The primary school teacher training course lasts for two years and includes the teaching of all primary school subjects. They are not specially trained to teach English; no help is given with the teaching of the script of English which is totally different from that of Gujarati.

**Classroom Behaviour**.
Many teachers are very reluctant to teach English as they have no confidence in their ability to speak it or teach it. They use Gujarati all of the time. The text books which are available are 1960's structurally based books. Classroom activities will usually consist of:
(a)   reading aloud in turn
(b)   mechanical drilling
(c)   copying sentences from the blackboard.

**Class Size** - about 70 pupils.
Imagine you are asked to indicate what recommendations you would make about helping these teachers who are reluctant and unhappy about teaching English to train pupils to use English for ordinary everyday classroom management tasks in these scenarios.

In this situation there is an added resource: there is a weekly programme on local radio on the teaching of English. It is late at night and poorly advertised. Hardly any of the teachers have ever heard about these radio programmes. These programmes were made at the local university with KELT officer working on the project so they are worth listening to.

**Scenario 1**
You have 2 days of inservice input per year and a very small sum of money.

**Scenario 2**
You have one week of inservice per year and rather more money than in one above but still a realistic amount for a developing country.

Imagine you are the local VSO. You have got 34 teachers of primary 4 (ages 9-12) in your area. You have decided to work with the teachers at this level. Would you concentrate on:
(1)   improving their language knowledge.
(2)   raising awareness of the relevant pedagogic skills.
(3)   altering attitudes to learner participation.
(4)   all of these?

INDICATE AS PRECISELY AS POSSIBLE WHAT YOU WOULD DO TO HELP THESE TEACHERS USING FIRST SCEN ARIO 1 AND SECONDLY SCENARIO 2.YOU SHOULD MAKE AT LEAST **THREE** RECOMMENDATIONS FOR EACH SCENARIO.

# Teacher training in the Sabah Primary English Programme

David Hayes

## ■ The new primary school curriculum – Kurikulum Baru Sekolah Rendah (KBSR)

In the early eighties the Malaysian Ministry of Education began the process of changing the curriculum in primary schools throughout the country. As far as English was concerned, this meant that teachers had to change from a structural syllabus and a 'traditional' methodology (teacher-centred with much choral repetition and formal grammatical exercises) to a skills-based syllabus and a 'communicative' methodology, with learner-centred classrooms where children engaged in activities suited to their conceptual level and which required them to use language for a purpose.

KBSR meant a radical change for primary school teachers of English.

How did the Ministry propose to effect these far-reaching changes, to ensure that teachers were sufficiently creative and independent to be able to implement the new syllabus for English?

KBSR was introduced progressively, starting with Primary 1 in 1983 and reaching Primary 6 in 1988. The strategies for its implementation were what Chin and Benne, cited in Kennedy (1987), call 'power-coercive' and 'rational-empirical'. Power-coercive in that the government required all schools to change to the new curriculum by law; and rational-empirical in that a series of orientation courses were held to provide teachers with information about the new curriculum and to convince them of its educational merits.

## ■ KBSR courses: the rational-empirical strategy for change

The nature, scope and content of these courses was determined by the Ministry. Every state sent three or four specialists for each subject to a course in Kuala Lumpur where, in effect, they received 'the message' about KBSR for their subject. They went back and organised courses for key personnel from each division in their states to pass on that message. The key personnel in turn organised courses for teachers of whatever year was being dealt with.

In practical terms, in a week-long course for teachers devoted to the entire curriculum for each year, English would be allotted seven hours for training. Given the fundamental nature of the change that was being attempted, this was clearly insufficient. It is no surprise to learn, therefore, that in Sabah, probably the least developed of the Malaysian states, the Department of Education (a division of the Federal Ministry) soon recognised that KBSR English was not, generally, being taught in schools as was intended, and saw an urgent need for further training for teachers.

## ■ The KELT Project and the Rural Primary English Programme

The Sabah KELT Project is responding to that need. Like all KELT projects (or simply ELT projects as they have now become), it is funded by the Overseas Development Administration (ODA) and administered by the British Council. The project is currently developing the Sabah Rural Primary English Programme (RuPEP). Although we will eventually cover all primary schools in the state, our first concern is with schools outside the three main urban centres, those schools in rural areas that usually get left behind in the development process.

RuPEP was originally conceived of by others as a direct teacher-training programme. Now, with due consideration given to programme sustainability and the need to involve teachers at the grass roots level in its development, it is evolving into a teacher-development programme. We have not excluded direct teacher-training courses run by non-school staff but these are now simply a means to another end. RuPEP in any division in the state now operates like this:

1   KELT (+ VSO if available) select two counterparts from schools – the Divisional Language Instructors (Div LIs).
2   They initiate a series of in-service teacher-training courses using KELT produced materials. The Div LIs are given on-the-job training via these courses and materials.
3   'Good' teachers from the courses are selected to act as trainers/group leaders – District Language Instructors (Dis LIs).
4   KELT/Div LIs give additional training to Dis LIs to enable them to teach elements of the in-service teacher-training courses. KELT/Div LIs supervise.
5   After the first series of courses (3 x 15 hours per term), Dis LIs receive training in preparing one-day workshops for teachers. The topic of the first workshop is chosen by KELT/Div LIs. Dis LIs are closely guided in constructing the workshop.
6   Dis LIs run the workshops (7/8 hours, once per term). KELT/Div LIs are available in an advisory rather than supervisory capacity.
7   Dis LIs select the topic for the next termly workshop based on their own analysis of teachers' needs. Div LIs are guided by KELT in preparing a training session for Dis LIs to enable the latter to construct/run the workshop.
8   Dis LIs select the topic for a further workshop in the same way. Div LIs prepare a training session to enable them to construct/run the workshop. KELT is available in an advisory capacity.
9   Dis LIs prepare workshops to respond to the expressed needs of their own groups of teachers. Div LIs assist and guide as necessary.
10  Teachers groups function virtually independently as self-help groups. They simply inform Div LIs what they intend to do, using Div LIs as a resource if they so wish.

Co-ordination and exchange of information/ideas between divisions is a continuing activity: this is a state-wide programme.

I would now like to examine our approaches to teacher training and the progression to teacher development.

## ■ RuPEP and teacher-training approaches

What we have to aim at in all of our training is an ideal as represented by KBSR: this is a given. If we look at aspects of our training in terms of a series of continua, KBSR characteristics will be at the right hand end – 'desirable' behaviour. At the other end we have the antitheses, behaviour that is 'undesirable' when viewed from the KBSR perspective.

    Within the classroom we need to take account of:

*Modes of learning*
Rote _____ Discovery

*Modes of teaching*
Teacher-centre _____ Learner-centred

*Teacher autonomy*
Dependent/imitative _____ Independent/creative

For our programme two other dimensions from outside the classroom are also relevant:

*Modes of training*
Lecture/deductive _____ Experiential/inductive

*Motivation for change*
Extrinsic _____ Intrinsic

In fact, these latter dimensions also reflect KBSR practice. In Sabah, if children are to learn English successfully their motivation has to be largely integrative (intrinsic) and KBSR posits that they 'acquire' the language through experiencing it in use.

    From intensive classroom observation we found that, for the most part, teachers were far from the KBSR ideal, being near or at the left hand end of each continuum. To achieve the KBSR ideal from this starting point is not an easy task. We have to ensure that any change that teachers make is deep-seated; that they change because they see that when they use the new methodology their children learn more effectively. Teachers have to be convinced that what KBSR asks them to do is right. As Prabhu (1987) puts it, we have to engage teachers' 'sense of plausibility' about what constitutes good, effective teaching and learning.

    Development of a sense of plausibility about teaching techniques can be likened to use of Chin and Benne's third strategy for implementing innovation: the 'normative-re-educative', underlying which 'is the idea that people act according to the values and attitudes prevalent in a given society or culture, and that accepting change may require changes to deep-seated beliefs and behaviour' (Kennedy, *op.cit.*, p. 164).

Normative-re-educative strategies and the notion of a sense of plausibility both inform our approach to teacher training and thence teacher development, though, obviously, we must work within the framework of KBSR. Rejection of its approaches, no matter how reasoned the rejection might be, cannot be considered a legitimate option for Sabah teachers.

Our starting place has, therefore, always been the teachers' present point of development (for practical purposes this obviously has to be generalised) and we hope to move from the 'undesirable' to the 'desirable' in incremental steps, a strategy of 'gradual approximation' to the ideal.

We need to take particular account at the outset of our teachers' previous training experiences and try to ensure that we meet their needs as learners/trainees.

Let us now see how these perceptions translate into practical training sessions.

### ■ Teacher-training sessions: the approaches exemplified

In all of our teacher-training sessions we have tried to encompass three elements and we encourage our Divisional and District LIs also to take account of them in the workshops they produce. These are:

1 Awareness
2 Methodology
3 Language improvement

Topics for sessions come from the following areas:

1 Listening
2 Speaking
3 Reading
4 Writing
5 Classroom language
6 The classroom environment

KBSR sees teaching/learning in terms of the 'four skills' and this also accords very much with teachers' existing perceptions. These topic areas cannot, in practice, be discrete and in any of them we are also able to focus on aspects of classroom management (organising groups/pairs for productive practice), which is an expressed need of the teachers.

Let us look at one of the skills areas – *Reading* – starting at the left hand end of the continua. The following could be said to be a 'reading' lesson typical of those found in many of Sabah's schools.

Lesson Report

The teacher goes into the classroom, asks children to take out their textbooks and open them at page ... S/he then says 'Read after me ...' The teacher reads a phrase, the children repeat it chorally. After the whole passage is read in this way, the procedure is repeated with children reading aloud in groups and individually. Five minutes before the end of the lesson the teacher asks the children to take out their exercise books and to do the comprehension questions which follow the reading passage. This has to be finished for homework.

How do we deal with this?

### Awareness-raising

We need first of all to 'activate' teachers' existing knowledge and perceptions about teaching and lead them to examine their own practice. One way of doing this is to list some techniques, both 'good' and 'bad', and then to ask teachers to say how often they use them in their classes (see Fig. 1).

Without referring back to their frequency check, teachers are next asked to say whether they think the same techniques are effective or ineffective. They then compare their two lists. Often teachers find that they say they are using techniques which they have rated 'not effective' and not using ones they have rated 'effective'. Lively group discussions can result from this as teachers explore the reasons behind their views and try to justify their use of techniques. At this stage tutors do not say that anything is the 'right way' to do something.

Fig. 1.                                                        Reading
Comprehension

## Worksheet 2:

## Teaching Techniques

How do you teach reading in your classes? Look at the list of techniques used in reading lessons. Which ones do you use? Put a tick ( ) against A (= Always) or S (= Sometimes) or N )= Never) according to how often you use the technique in your reading lessons.

| No. | Technique | A | S | N |
|-----|-----------|---|---|---|
| 1. | Teacher uses English only in the lesson | | | |
| 2. | Teacher and children use Bahasa Malaysia as well as English in the lesson. | | | |
| 3. | First reading: children follow while teacher reads aloud. | | | |
| 4. | First reading: children read silently and answer 2 or 3 simple questions. | | | |

### *Methodology*

Teachers can then be led to 'discover' the 'right way' according to KBSR by comparing and anlaysing reports of two lessons – one good, one bad. They extract lesson plans from the reports, focusing on teacher activity, pupil activity and the aims of the activities. In one lesson they should see that the activities children engage in are meaningless, have no purpose; in the other that activities are meaningful with children being helped to read with understanding.

In the early stages of the programme we tend to take something that teachers are generally doing badly in their classes when we first observe them and try to show them how to do it better. The break with a past practice and experience cannot be immediate or too radical as (a) teachers need time to understand and assimilate fully new techniques; and (b) they have a personal investment in that previous experience. We cannot expect immediate self-denial of perhaps years of teaching experience.

### *Language improvement*

This is a sensitive area. We have come under pressure to include direct language improvement sessions in our courses. There is little doubt that many teachers' command of English is very poor. Equally, there are others whose command of the language is excellent; and often these two extremes are to be found in the same group of teachers.

But the desire for these language improvement sessions is founded on a basic misapprehension, which is that more competent speakers of the language are necessarily more competent teachers of it. Our extensive classroom observation supports the view that this is not the case. Concentration on language improvement may also be counter-productive in that it can make teachers very aware of their limitations rather than any strengths.

Our preferred practice is for language improvement to be dealt with incidentally in methodology sessions. Methodology is not dealt with in the abstract. All of these sessions feature use of KBSR teachers' guides, textbooks and teaching/learning aids for demonstration, analysis, lesson planning and peer micro-teaching purposes. So in methodology sessions teachers have the opportunity to use the language that, at some stage, they will have to teach to their classes. The focus on groupwork in teacher-training sessions also provides a chance for teachers whose English is weak to learn from those who are more proficient. Tutors have the additional option of making specific comments in passing about the language to whole groups or to individual teachers if they feel it necessary.

### ■ **Moving along the continua: reading**

From concentration on improvement of existing practice, which at the same time sensitises teachers to the principles underlying the practice, we are able to move gradually to innovations from KBSR. As we move along the continua, as it were, we are also able to lay increasing stress on the fact that teachers are dealing with children.

To take an example. In Sandakan division we first looked at 'Reading Comprehension' for upper primary classes: now the Divisional LIs are preparing a course for District LIs to construct a workshop on reading storybooks to children.

### Awareness-raising

As part of our awareness-raising strategy we will video one of the Divisional LIs teaching a lesson and ask teachers to view it and complete an observation checklist. This will lead them to reconsider earlier basic points about the importance of teaching reading with understanding, preparing children by talking about the topic, drawing on children's own experience, and so on. Recycling and reinforcement is crucial. We will also show a video of a teacher in a British primary school telling a story to her class: teachers view and complete the same observation checklist. We do not expect them to replicate British experience but it provides a stimulus for reflection and reinforces points about engaging the children's minds, use of prediction, appropriacy of language and use of visuals.

### Methodology

In practice Divisional and District LIs will already have decided what can be done within KBSR limits. We will ask teachers to look at pages from KBSR teachers' guides to extract the recommendations for reading and then show a third video, this time of one of our District LIs reading a story to her class, using the 'Big Book' approach. Teachers will be asked to analyse this via the observation checklist which will serve to re-emphasise points made earlier. This video will also demonstrate to teachers that the approach is feasible in Sabah's schools and that reading stories does make learning much more fun for children provided that it is done properly. As well as why teachers should read to children, how to read 'properly' can be deduced from the video and from a booklet – 'Reading Storybooks' – prepared by a British volunteer formerly working on the project. This booklet gives advice on how to make 'Big Books', in addition to describing how and why to use them. Part of the workshop will be practical, with groups writing stories, making books and practising using them with their peers. Stressing the need for teachers to work co-operatively to produce reading materials for their schools and to ensure maximum use of resources already in schools (such as books recently supplied as part of a World Bank programme) is also important.

In all of this a key part is played by District LIs and it is to consideration of features of their own training that I will now turn.

### ■ RuPEP and trainer-training approaches

In RuPEP we have to identify early on those teachers whom we think have the potential to become group leaders. Our choice is subjective and based on classroom performance as well as course performance.

Trainer training has to develop from our teacher-training approaches if we are to reach the goal of District LIs becoming group leaders who assist teachers in achieving effective self-development. Many teachers in Sabah's schools sense that their pedagogic intuition is somehow inadequate (as they realise that children are not learning) but they have no means of escaping from their predicament: the primary job of District LIs, therefore, is to help them clear the obstacles to progress. This is, of course, easier said than done and the task facing District LIs is, in many respects, daunting. They will have been selected on the basis that their classroom practice approximates more closely to KBSR than others and they will have shown themselves receptive to new ideas as participants on our teacher-training courses; they will also have been seen to be natural leaders of groups, assisting but not dominating their peers. However, to move from that to becoming virtually autonomous teacher trainers is a big step. Consider some of the elements that need to be taken account of when putting together a workshop for teachers:

- Identifying problems.
- Identifying solutions.
- Presenting a problem as a meaningful activity for teachers to solve.
- Selecting appropriate input.
- Devising/grading tasks.
- Ensuring utilisation of teachers' prior knowledge and skills.
- Ensuring worthwhile outcomes.

This list is far from exhaustive and within any one of these areas a multitude of skills and sub-skills needs to be mastered.

The idea of 'gradual approximation' which informs our teacher training also informs our trainer training. When we first give training courses for District LIs they will have had no experience of either running or creating workshops for teachers. As initial fears of these teacher trainers-to-be are largely concerned with 'How am I going to face a group of my fellow teachers?', it is with workshop management techniques that we start and the crutch of KELT-prepared materials with detailed tutor's notes is provided. The training methodology for District LIs will, then, be something like this (the needs of District LIs in all the divisions may not be the same, so there can be variation from division to division):

1  Dis LIs undergo training (c. 25 hours in school holidays) to enable them to teach KELT-produced materials. Focus on workshop management skills. Materials analysed also for underlying methodological principles.

2  Supervised teaching with prepared materials.

3  Unsupervised teaching with prepared materials. This provides an opportunity for self-reflection and the chance to experiment with the materials to a limited degree.

4  Further training (c. 25 hours) with focus shifted to workshop construction. Problem identified, Dis LIs look at possible solutions, course aims, creating meaningful tasks/worksheets for teachers.

5  Running workshops (one day) with Div LIs/KELT as advisors only.

6  Further training (c. 25 hours) with continued focus on aspects of workshop construction – forms of input for tasks, variety of tasks, ensuring teachers' prior knowledge and skills utilised.

7  Running workshops (one day per term).

Steps 6 – 7 repeated to end of project with increasing focus on workshops as vehicles for teacher self-development.

## ■ Conclusion

It is too early to claim success for our approach and, in any case, the true measure of any success will only be apparent after the end of the KELT project, in the activity that continues when all British personnel have been withdrawn. From the evidence that we have so far, we believe that we are working along the right lines. Our District LIs are already more self-confident, more knowledgeable, more aware. The teachers that they are beginning to work with in their groups are also becoming more alive and responsive to the demands of KBSR. There is still a long way to go, however, and the danger of regression will be ever-present until the shared expectations of both teachers and learners as to what constitutes 'English lessons' in Sabah's primary schools are firmly fixed along the child-centred, activity-oriented lines of KBSR.

I am aware that there are many aspects of a programme concerned with 2,000 or so teachers and 150 trainers that I have been unable to deal with in this paper – the nature of counterparting for Divisional LIs and the role of supervision/observation for District LIs and teachers, for example. And the Rural Primary English Programme is, in itself, but one factor in the equation. The crucial part in the implementation of KBSR that has to be played by headteachers, school supervisors and the schools' inspectorate also has to be recognised. However, our hope is that with the approaches we have adopted and the systems that we have set up we can help some of Sabah's teachers towards continuing self-development.

### Notes

The views expressed in this paper are those of the author and not necessarily those of ODA.

The author would like to acknowledge support from ODA which made possible his attendance at the BAAL/CBT seminar on Primary ELT.

# *Post-script*

At the end of the Conference at which the papers in this Collection were first presented, all Conference participants were invited to come together to discuss the issues which the Conference had raised and those which should be further addressed. This post-script is intended to outline the main questions that concerned the participants at that time. What follows below is not an exhaustive overview and readers will no doubt have other issues to add both from their own reading of this Collection and from their experience.

1  Policy decisions on the introduction of Primary level English language may be taken without clear ideas of how policy will be implemented or the constraints placed on implementation. Educational thinking needs to inform the decision-making process so that correct decisions are taken. Remaining points below illustrate some of the issues that need to be taken into account.

2  The theoretical justification for English for young learners is still not clear. Benefits may be claimed on cultural, cognitive or linguistic grounds. It should be made clear which of these arguments is being used to justify programmes. More research is required to support or counter the claims made by proponents of schemes.

3  The question of resources is important. We need to know not only whether there is an appropriate time to introduce English for the younger learner but also how much time should be devoted to it and whether it should be regarded as a separate subject on the curriculum or integrated with other learning. Some teachers work in physically under-resourced situations and are at a loss to see how the more interactive approaches advocated by some practitioners can be implemented with little equipment and large classes. The most valuable resource to be considered is the teacher (see point 8 below).

4  We should strive to see similarities between what might at first sight appear to be different situations and resist the desire to compartmentalise different aspects of Primary level work. On the other hand, differences where they exist should be recognised and their influence on the design of programmes acknowledged. For example, the specific roles and functions of English in a country normally have considerable impact on the motivation of pupils. However, at Primary level, pupil motivation is likely to be driven by immediate learning rather than by extrinsic considerations. The EFL/ESL distinctions (and the different interpretations of what is meant by ESL) need to be looked at with greater care and their implications for curriculum design assessed carefully.

5  The EFL/ESL distinction may be less significant in the design of programmes than other variables that have been identified as important. Physical resources have already been mentioned (point 3 above); degree of central control over syllabus and examinations, and cultural attitudes to teaching and learning are others.

6   The question of transfer of methods and materials from one context to another needs to be investigated (especially since approaches may be promoted with little evidence of their long-term success or failure). Transfer may be possible and any natural resistance to change overcome. On the other hand more fundamental problems may exist which prevent transfer (such as those mentioned in point 5 above). Investigation of what actually happens in Primary level classrooms is required, and why certain events occur and which practices are the most effective.

7   Language learning at Primary level is intricately bound up with the physical and natural development of the child and is clearly an educational undertaking. Primary ELT should therefore draw on a wide range of sources of information, including cognitive psychology and mother tongue teaching, for guidance and inspiration. In English medium situations it will need to justify its existence as a separate subject on the curriculum rather than as part of an integrated Primary syllabus.

8   The teacher plays a crucial role in the success or failure of programmes at this level. Many questions are still to be resolved about teacher training. Linguistic confidence appears to be a vital element without which Primary level teachers find it difficult to put their skills into practice. The question of appropriate training is important and there is much discussion whether we should be training Primary teachers who need a linguistic boost or language teachers who need training in Primary level techniques. It is unwise to be dogmatic about this and different contexts will produce different solutions, but opinion at the moment appears to be supporting the former profile.

Chris Kennedy
Jennifer Jarvis

# Bibliography

Abrahams, E. (ed.), 1986. *Topiwala the Hatmaker*, Harmony Publishing , Stanmore, Middlesex

Allwright, D., 1984a. 'Why Don't Learners Learn What Teachers Teach? – The Interaction Hypothesis' in Singleton, D.M. and D.G. Little (eds.), *Language Learning in Formal and Informal Contexts*, IRAAL, Dublin

Allwright, D., 1984b, 'The Importance of Interaction in Classroom Language Learning', *Applied Linguistics*, 5.2, pp.156-171

Allwright, D., 1988, *Observation in the Language Classroom*, Longman

Arora, T. and J. Bamford, 1986, 'M.A.T.H.S. – Multiply Attainments Through Home Support: Piloting "Paired Number" in an Infant School', *Educational and Child Psychology*, 3,3, pp. 68–74

Baker, C., 1988, *Key Issues in Bilingualism and Bilingual Education*, Multilingual Matters, Clevedon

Barnes, D. and F. Todd, 1977, *Communication and Learning in Small Groups*, Routledge and Kegan Paul

Bloor, M. (1992), 'The Role of Informal Interaction in Teaching English to Young Learners' in Brumfit, C. (ed.), *Teaching English to Young Learners,* Collins

Brewster, J., 1987, 'Co-operation and Control: A Study of Interactional Strategies Used in Task-based Collaborative Learning in the Primary School' (unpublished M. Phil. thesis, University of Birmingham)

Britten, D., 1985, 'Teacher Training in ELT (Part 2)', *Language Teaching,* July 1985, pp. 220–238

Brock, C.A., 1986, 'The Effects of Referential Questions on ESL Classroom Discourse', *TESOL Quarterly*, 20, pp. 47–59

Brumfit, C., 1979, 'Notional Syllabuses: A Reassessment', *System*, 7.2

Burstall, C., 1968, *French from Eight: A National Experiment*, NFER, Slough

Burstall, C., 1970, *French in the Primary School: Attitudes and Achievements*, NFER, Slough

Burstall, C. et al., 1974, *Primary French in the Balance*, NFER, Slough

Byrne, D. and M. Palmer, 1982, *Track 1*, Longman

Candlin, C., 1988, preface to Allwright, *Observation in the Language Classroom,* op. cit.

*Centre Well: Listening Comprehension, Information Transfer, Process Writing*, Centre for British Teachers Publications, Brunei

Chambers, R., 1983, *Rural Development: Putting the Last First*, Longman

Chatwin, R., 1988, 'Which Way for ESL?' *Multicultural Education Review, 8*

Chaudron, Craig, 1988, 'Classroom Research: Recent Methods and Findings', *AILA Review,* 5

Christopherson, P., 1972, *Second Language Learning.* Harmondsworth: Penguin

Clark, J., 1987, *Curriculum Renewal in School Foreign Language Learning,* Oxford University Press

Clarke, D.F., 1989, 'Communication Theory and its Influence on Materials Production', *Language Teaching*, Cambridge University Press

Coleman, H., 1989a, *The Study of Large Classes* (Project Report No. 2), Lancaster-Leeds Language Learning in Large Classes Research Project, Leeds University

Coleman, H., 1989b, *Large Classes in Nigeria* (Project Report No. 6), Lancaster-Leeds Language Learning in Large Classes Research Project, Leeds University

Coleman, H., 1989c, 'The Relationship Between Large Class Research and Large Class Teaching' (paper presented at the 5th Annual Seminar of SPELT – Society of Pakistan English Language Teachers – Karachi, October 1989)

Constable, P., 1985, 'Planning the Primary School Syllabus', *ETAZ Journal,* 9.1, Educational Services, Lusaka

Coventry College of Education, 1967, *Primary School French – Advice to School Practice Tutors* (unpublished)

Crombie, W., 1988, 'Syllabus and Method: System or Licence?', *System,* 16.3

Crystal, D., 1987, *Child Language, Learning and Linguistics,* 2nd edn., Edward Arnold

Cummins, J., 1980, 'The Cross-lingual Dimensions of Language Proficiency; Implications for Bilingual Education and the Optimal Age Issue' in *TESOL Quarterly* 14.2

Cummins, J., 1984, 'Wanted: A Theoretical Framework for Relating Language Proficiency to Academic Achievement among Bilingual Students' in Rivera, C. (ed.), *Language Proficiency and Academic Achievement,* Multilingual Matters, Cleveland

Cunningsworth, A., 1987, 'Coursebooks and Conversational Skills' in Sheldon, L. (ed.), *ELT Textbooks: Problems in Evaluation and Development,* Modern English Publications

Dallas, D. and R. Williams, 1984, 'Aspects of Vocabulary in the Readability of Content Area L2 Educational Testbooks: A Case Study' in Alderson, J.C. and A. Urquhart (eds.), *Reading in a Foreign Language,* Longman

Department of Education and Science, 1975, *A Language for Life* ('The Bullock Report'), HMSO

Department of Education and Science, 1988, *English for Ages 5–11* ('The Cox Report') HMSO

Donaldson, Margaret, 1978, *Children's Minds,* Collins/Fontana

Dulay, H. *et al.*, 1982, *Language Two*, Oxford University Press

Dunn, O., 1983, *Beginning English with Young Learners*, Macmillan

Dunn, O., 1985, *Developing English with Young Learners*, Macmillan

Elliot, A., 1981, *Child Language*, Cambridge University Press

Ellis, G. and B. Sinclair, 1989, *Learning to Learn English – A Course in Learner Training,* Cambridge University Press

Ellis, R., 1984, *Classroom Second Language Development,* Pergamon

Fanselow, J.F., 1977, 'Beyond Rashomon – Conceptualising and Describing the Teaching Act', *TESOL Quarterly,* 11.1, pp. 17–39

Garvey, C., 1975, 'Requests and Responses in Children's Speech', *Journal of Child Language,* 6

Garvie, E., 1976, *Breakthrough to Fluency,* Basil Blackwell

Garvie, E., 1990, *Story as Vehicle: Teaching English to Young Children,* Multilingual Matters, Clevedon

Gaudart, H., 1989, in Krishnades, K. (ed.), *KBSMM English,* Form 2, Federal Publications, Malaysia

Genesee, F., 1978, 'Is there an optimal age for starting second language instruction?' *McGill Journal of Education* 13, pp. 145–154

Graves, D., 1983, *Writing: Teachers and Children at Work,* Heinemann

Hannon, P. and A. Jackson, 1987, *The Belfield Reading Project Final Report,* Belfield County Council in association with the National Children's Bureau

Harley, B., 1986, *Age in Second Language Acquisition,* Clevedon: Multilingual Matters

Harding, E. and P. Riley, 1986, *The Bilingual Family,* Cambridge University Press

Hatch, E., 1983, *Psycholinguistics, a second language perspective,* Rowley, MA: Newbury House

Hawkes, N., 1981, 'Primary Children' in Johnson K. and K. Morrow (eds.), *Communication in the Classroom,* Longman

Hawkes, N., Iyabode Macaulay and D. Dallas, 1977–81, *Nigeria Primary English 1–6,* Longman for Longman Nigeria

Hewison, J. and J. Tizard, 1980, 'Parental Involvement and Reading Attainment', *British Journal of Educational Psychology,* 50, pp. 209–215

HMSO, 1967, *Children and their Primary Schools* ('The Plowden Report'), HMSO

Houlton, D. and R. Willey, 1983, *Supporting Children's Bilingualism,* Longman for the Schools Council

Hughes, G.S., 1981, *A Handbook of Classroom English,* Oxford University Press

Hutchinson, T., 1987, 'What's Underneath? An Interactive View of Materials Evaluation' in Sheldon, L. (ed.), *ELT Textbooks: Problems in Evaluation and Development,* Modern English Publications

Ickes, W. and R. Barnes, 1978, 'Boys and Girls Together – and Alienated: On Enacting Stereotyped Sex-roles in Mixed-sex Dyads', *Journal of Personality and Social Psychology,* 36.7

Johnson, K., 1981, *Communicative Syllabus Design and Methodology,* Pergamon

Johnson, K., 1983, *Now for English 1*, Nelson

Kellermann, M., 1981, *The Forgotten Third Skill: Reading a Foreign Language,* Pergamon

Kementerian Pelajaran Malaysia, 1982, *Buku Panduan Khas: Bahasa Inggeris, Tahun Satu,* Dewan Bahasa dan Pustaka, Kuala Lumpur

Kementerian Pelajaran Malaysia, 1983, *Buku Panduan Khas: Bahasa Inggeris, Tahun Dua,* Dewan Bahasa dan Pustaka, Kuala Lumpur

Kementerian Pelajaran Malaysia, 1984, *Buku Panduan Khas: Bahasa Inggeris, Tahun Tiga,* Dewan Bahasa dan Pustaka, Kuala Lumpur

Kennedy, C., 1987, 'Innovating for a Change: Teacher Development and Innovation', *ELT Journal,* 41.3, pp. 163–170

Lenneberg, E., 1967, *Biological Foundations of Language,* New York: John Wiley

LoCastro, Virginia, 1989, *Large Size Classes: The Situation in Japan* (Project Report No. 5), Lancaster-Leeds Language Learning in Large Classes Research Project, Leeds University

Marland, M., 1987, *Multilingual Britain – The Educational Challenge,* CILT

Medgyes, P., 1986, 'Queries from a Communicative Teacher' *English Language Teaching Journal,* 40.2

Miller, J., 1983, *Many Voices: Bilingualism, Culture and Education,* Routledge and Kegan Paul

Mills, D. *et al.*, 1971, *English for French Speaking Africa,* Students Book 2, *Enjoy Learning English 5e,* Armand Collins

Morgan, R. and E. Lyon, 1979, 'Paired Reading', *Journal of Child Psychology and Psychiatry,* 20

Munby, J., 1978, *Communicative Syllabus Design,* Cambridge University Press

NCC, 1989, *National Curriculum Council Consultation Report: English 5–11,* York: NCC

Nesbit, J. and J. Shucksmith, 1986, *Learning Strategies,* Routledge and Kegan Paul

Oduol, Charles, 1987, 'Maintenance of Communication in Primary Classrooms: Some Evidence for the Role of Elicitation and Code-switching in English Medium Schools in Kenya' (PhD thesis, Aston University, Birmingham)

O'Neill, R., 1978, *Kernel One,* Longman

Peachey, L., 1989, *Language Learning in Large Classes: A Pilot Study of South African Data* (Project Report No. 8), Lancaster-Leeds Language Learning in Large Classes Research Project, Leeds University

Phillips, T., 1985, 'Beyond Lip-service: Discourse Development after the Age of Nine' in Wells, C.G. and J. Nicholls, *Language and Learning: An Interactional Perspective,* Falmer Press

Pica, T. and C. Doughty, 1985, 'The Role of Groupwork in Classroom Second Language Acquisition', *Studies in Second Language Acquisition,* 7.2, Cambridge University Press

Prabhu, N.S., 1987, *Second Language Pedagogy,* Oxford University Press

Pratt, C., A. Garton, W. Tunmer and A. Nesdale, 1986, *Research Issues in Child Development,* Allen and Unwin

Pride, J.B., 1983, 'Stylistic Variation in the Repertoire of the Bilingual/Multilingual Speaker', *RELC Journal* (Singapore), 14.1

Primary Certificate of Education Exams, 1989, Examinations Board, Ministry of Education, Brunei

Prodromou, Luke, 1988, 'English as Cultural Action', *ELT Journal,* 42.2, pp. 73–83

Pugh, G., 1981, *Parents as Partners,* National Children's Bureau, London

Renshaw, P. and A. Garton, 1986, 'Children's Collaboration and Conflict in Dyadic Problem Solving' in Pratt, C. *et al., Research Issues in Child Development,* Allen and Unwin

Revised Primary English Syllabus and Primary History Syllabus for Brunei Darussalam, 1989, Curriculum Development Department, Ministry of Education, Brunei Darussalam

Reynolds, M., J., 1989, 'Repair and Control in the Native Speaker/Non-native Speaker Classroom' (PhD thesis, University of Lancaster)

Robinson, E. and W. Robinson, 1982, 'The Advancement of Children's Verbal Referential Communication Skills: The Role of Metacognitive Guidance', *International Journal of Behavioural Development,* 5

Rogers, R. (ed.), 1980, *Crowther to Warnock: How Fourteen Reports Tried to Change Children's Lives,* Heinemann Educational Books

Rosen, B., 1988, *And None of it was Nonsense,* Mary Glasgow Publications

Rubin, J., 1977, 'Textbook Writers and Language Planning' in Rubin J. *et al.* (eds.), *Language Planning Processes,* Mouton, The Hague

Sabandar, Jacob, 1989, *Language Learning in Large Classes in Indonesia* (Project Report No. 9), Lancaster-Leeds Language Learning in Large Classes Research Project, Leeds University

Sarangi, Usha, 1989, *A Consideration of Methodological Issues in Analysing the Problems of Language Teachers in Large Classes* (Project Report No. 10), Lancaster-Leeds Language Learning in Large Classes Research Project, Leeds University

Schofield, W., 1979, *Haringey Reading Project Final Report,* Thomas Coram Research for the Department of Education and Science, London

Schools Council, 1966, *French in the Primary School,* HMSO

Schools Council, 1966-1967, *En Avant* 1A, 1B, 2, E. G. Arnold, Leeds

Schumann, J., 1975, 'Affective factors and the problem of age in second language acquistion', *Language Learning* 25, pp. 209–235

Serpell, R., 1980a, 'The Cultural Context of Language Learning: Problems Confronting English Teachers in Zambia' (paper presented to the Annual Conference of the English Teachers' Association of Zambia)

Serpell, R., 1980b, 'Linguistic Flexibility in Urban Zambian School Children', in Teller, V. and S.J. White (eds.), *Studies in Child Language and Bilingualism,* Annals of the New York Academy of Science, 345, pp. 97–119

Sinclair, J. McH, and R.M. Coulthard, 1975, *Towards an Analysis of Discourse,* Oxford University Press

Singleton, D., 1989, *Language Acquisition: the age factor,* Clevedon: Multilingual Matters

Smith, P., 1985, *Language, the Sexes and Society,* Basil Blackwell

Strevens, P., 1981, 'Forms of English: an Analysis of the Variables', in Smith, L.E. (ed.), *English for Cross-Cultural Communication,* Macmillan

Stubbs, Michael, 1983, *Discourse Analysis,* Blackwell

Stubbs, Michael, 1986, *Educational Linguistics,* Blackwell

Swan, M., 1985, 'A Critical Look at the Communicative Approach, 1–2', *English Language Teaching Journal,* 39, pp. 1–2

Titone, R., 1986, 'Un passaporto per il futuro', *L'Educatore* 34, 6, pp. 4–9

Thorne, B. and N. Henley, 1975, *Language and Sex: Difference and Dominance,* Newbury House

Ur, P., 1981, *Discussions that Work,* Cambridge University Press

van Ek, J., 1975, *Threshold Level,* Council of Europe

Vygotsky, L., 1978, *Mind in Society,* Harvard University Press

Wagner-Gough, J & E Hatch 1975, 'The importance of input data in second language acquisition studies', *Language Learning* 25, pp. 297–308

Waterland, L., 1985, *Read with Me, An Apprenticeship Approach to Reading,* The Thimble Press

Waters, A., 1988, 'Teacher-training Course Design: A Case Study', *ELT Journal,* 42.1, pp. 14–19

Wells, C.G. and J.Nicholls (eds.), 1985, *Language Learning: An Interactional Perspective,* Falmer Press

Widdowson, H., 1985, 'Against Dogma: A Reply to Michael Swan', *English Language Teaching Journal,* 39.3

Wigzell, R., 1982, 'The Role and Status of English as a Subject in the Zambian English-Medium Context', in *ELT Documents 116: Language Teaching Projects for the Third World,* Pergamon/British Council

Willis, J., 1981, *Teaching English Through English,* Longman

Zambian Ministry of Education, 1977, 'Educational Reform: Proposals and Recommendations', Government Printers, Lusaka

Zawadzka, A. and E. Moszczak, 1982, *English is Fun,* WSiP

Zimmermann, D. and C. West, 1975, 'Sex Roles, Interruptions and Silences in Conversation' in Thorne, B. and N. Henley, *Language and Sex: Difference and Dominance,* Newbury House

# *Contributors*

**Meriel Bloor** is a lecturer at the Centre for English Language Teaching, University of Warwick. She has varied teaching experience, including three years in a British primary school and twelve years in Africa. She has published many articles and is co-author of *Tests in English as a Foreign Language* (Macmillan), *Reading for a Purpose* (Longman) and *New Primary English for Lesotho* (Longman).

**Jean Brewster** is Senior Lecturer in ELT at Ealing College of Higher Education, where she is involved in teacher training for teachers from all over the world. She has been Course Director, Chief Examiner and Assessor for the RSA Diploma in Teaching English Across the Curriculum, and has had considerable experience of primary-school-based teacher training projects in Language Across the Curriculum and Language Awareness. She has worked for the British Council on teacher training seminars in several countries, and has published articles on primary TEFL and language in education.

**Christopher Brumfit** is Professor of Education with reference to language and linguistics at the University of Southampton, UK. He has taught in primary and secondary schools in Britain and Africa, in a teacher training college in Birmingham, and in the Universities of Dar es Salaam and London, and has lectured or run workshops in most other parts of the world. He has published over twenty books on ELT, literature teaching and language in education.

**Hywel Coleman** trained as a primary teacher. His teaching career began in special education in England, after which he spent eleven years in Indonesia as an EFL teacher, materials writer and teacher trainer. He now teaches at the University of Leeds, where he co-ordinates the M.Ed.TESOL programme.

**Peta Constable** is at present an ODA-funded British Council ELT Adviser in Zambia; her paper is based on her work for the Zambia ELT Materials Writing and Methodology Project.

**Norma Dickinson** has worked in the Scottish Centre for Education Overseas, Moray House College, Edinburgh since 1978. Earlier she taught at the upper primary level in Spain and then at the Secondary and tertiary level in Scotland. Her main areas of interest are a) teacher education at primary and lower secondary levels, b) the teaching/learning of reading and writing, and c) the importance of language competence in selecting appropriate teaching methodologies.

**Opal Dunn** is a freelance consultant in bilingual education for children. She has worked with young learners and trained teachers of young learners both overseas and in Britain. She specialises in beginning English with young children and especially in the introduction of reading and writing in English. She has written materials for young beginners and teachers and is currently writing for parents and children learning English, as well as for native-speaking children.

**Reinhold Freudenstei**n is currently Professor of Education at Philipps University, Marburg, Germany, Director of the Foreign Language Research Information Centre at Marburg University and a member of the Executive Board of the World Federation of Modern Language Associations. His interests are European language policy, language teaching to young learners, teacher training, media use and testing.

**Edie Garvie** entered the field of EFL/ESL after many years of experience in the British (Scottish) mainstream primary school. She worked for five years in Uganda, training both primary and secondary teachers. Back in Britain, she became involved in the new multicultural scene in education, while at the same time gaining further overseas experience mainly in Southern Africa and Malaysia. She is now a freelance lecturer, writer and teacher trainer.

**Nicolas Hawkes** is Lecturer in Education at Stirling University, Scotland, and Director of the full-time in-service B.Ed. He has been a secondary teacher of English and British Council English Language Officer, mainly in Africa; researcher and materials developer in primary level ESL/EFL at York University; and was for three years Curriculum Adviser (Primary English) in Zimbabwe.

**David Hayes** is at present part of an ODA-funded British Council Advisory Team working on a primary English project for rural schools in Malaysia.

**Rosalyn Hurst** is Head of TESOL Section at the West Sussex Institute of Higher Education. She has taught in primary and secondary schools in Cameroon, Iran and the UK. She is now involved with teacher training programmes for both levels of teachers of English, both at the Institute and on in-service courses overseas.

**Jennifer Jarvis** is Lecturer in Education at Leeds University, where she has responsibility for ELT in-service teacher training courses. She travels widely as a teacher, trainer and consultant in ELT. Amongst other recent activities in the young learner field, she has directed the new British Council Summer School for Teachers of English to Young Learners.

**Chris Kennedy** was seconded from the University of Birmingham, where he is responsible for ELT Teacher Training Courses, to work as Chief Executive for the Centre for British Teachers from 1987 to 1990. His main interests are in language policy and ELT management and evaluation. He is currently Chairman of the International Association for Teachers of English as a Foreign Language.

**Julia Khan** is Joint Director of the Centre for English Language Teaching at the University of Warwick. She has long professional experience of language teaching and teacher training. Current research interests include the development of children's language skills in a bilingual context.

**Hugh Leburn's** early training and experience was in primary teaching in the UK. He has taught EFL to a wide range of students in Colombia, Finland and Malaysia. He was, for a number of years, Primary Adviser on the CBT Primary project in Brunei.

**Ludmila Machura** has had extensive experience as a teacher of English, from primary to university levels. She is currently a teacher and teacher trainer at the Institute of English, Warsaw University. She is also involved in primary teaching, and has particular interests in children's literature in ELT. She has published articles on testing, teacher development and teaching children.

**Bob Marsden** has been working at BBC English for nine years, first as a radio producer, now as a video and television producer. He has taught EFL in various countries, including primary schools in Sweden. He has also worked as a teacher trainer, especially in the use of media in teaching. He is the author of several EFL course books, including *Crossroads, Options, The Cambridge First Certificate Course* (Nelson), and *People and Places* (BBC English).

**Rosemary Scott** has a Masters Degree in Applied Linguistics. She is an RSA Dip TEFL Assessor and has been involved in English language teaching and teacher training in the UK and overseas. Her most recent publication is *Food for Thought*, an oral skills book which she co-authored for Penguin. She taught young learners in Bury for the English Language Teaching Service and is currently working for Haringey Language Resource Centre in London.